TABLE OF CONTENTS

Build your own Shed?

The answer is YES! By doing the planning and all or part of the work yourself, you can have the shed you might not otherwise be able to afford. By supplying the labor and buying materials yourself, construction costs can be cut significantly.

Framing out a shed is not difficult. Standardized materials and construction techniques make it relatively easy if you take time to plan and work carefully.

Planning your Shed

The key to a successful shed project is planning, planning, and more planning! Once you have begun construction of your shed, it is both costly and time-consuming to correct errors in shed placement, construction, or selection of materials. So the motto of the Do-It-Yourself shed builder must be **PLAN AHEAD!** Whether you choose to draw the plans for your shed following the guidelines in this manual or you decide to purchase a *UCANDO* shed plan which can be adapted to your unique requirements, you must carefully plan all elements of your shed project.

Here is a checklist of design information which you must gather ***before*** you begin to build:

Local Building Requirements. Visit your local building department and determine how local building codes and zoning ordinances will influence your project. Certain municipalities restrict the height, placement, and square footage of shed buildings. Be prepared to apply for a building permit once you have completed your design.

Deed Restrictions. Are there conditions in your property deed that restrict the type and location of your shed? Are you planning to place your shed over property controlled by an easement for right-of-way or utility access?

Climatic Factors. Evaluate the microclimate of your intended shed location. Microclimate includes the shading effects of deciduous or evergreen trees and shrubs, the angle of the sun in relation to nearby landscaping during different seasons, soil drainage conditions, and prevailing wind and temperature conditions. Remember that an enclosed shed without temperature regulation needs to be protected from the sun in the summer and exposed to any available sunlight in the winter.

Shed Functions. What do you want your shed to do? Will your shed serve as a simple storage building for gardening and lawn tools or do you plan to use the shed to store household items? Do you want to supply the shed with electrical power? What type of storage or shelving units would you like to install in your completed shed? Will your shed include a workshop or hobby area? Careful planning regarding the functions of your shed will save you from costly changes after the project is completed.

Plan carefully *before* you begin. All the techniques and tips you'll need are in this book. Read it carefully before you begin construction. It will help you determine the work you can handle alone and also where expert help might be needed to do the job right.

You can also learn many construction basics by studying existing sheds. Ask your neighbors if you can take a few minutes to review their shed before you begin planning your design.

Your Budget. You must determine an estimated dollar amount that you plan to spend on your shed. Do you plan to construct the shed yourself or will you subcontract with a professional to build the shed after you have purchased materials? Perhaps you want a contractor to complete your shed project in its entirety. It is helpful if you can set upper and lower spending limits so that you can consider options in the materials that you plan for your shed. If you decide to finance your shed project, don't forget to include interest cost in the total cost amount.

Your Materials Source. While many of you will shop different sources for materials after you have completed your design work and settled on a bill of materials, you should remember that a helpful lumber dealer or home center is an invaluable resource for the successful completion of your shed project. Consult with a dealer of your choice to be certain that they stock all the materials you require. If special ordering is necessary, determine lead times for the materials that the dealer does not carry in regular inventory. Check if the dealer can deliver materials directly to your site. Don't underestimate the importance of a reputable dealer in providing both quality materials and design knowledge.

Prefabricated or from scratch. You can purchase a prefabricated wood or metal shed in a limited variety of styles or you can obtain one of the *UCANDO* shed plans illustrated at the back of this manual. Remember that metal sheds are subject to wind damage and have a relatively short lifespan in comparison to wood sheds. If you do purchase a shed kit, this manual can still provide valuable assistance regarding construction techniques and materials. If you build from scratch, this manual is a complete guide to shed construction.

Planning Your Shed Continued

The shed site plans on this page are included to exemplify how your shed can contribute valuable storage space to your home. Before you place your shed on your property, study traffic patterns in your back yard and how often you will use the shed on a daily basis. Create a site plan of your property and draw arrows to illustrate the basic movements to and from your home. Establish priorities for storage locations and traffic to your proposed shed.

Be aware of problem areas that relate to shed placement. Will you need to build a ramp to move lawn tools in and out of the shed? Be certain that you have adequate clearances to move these tools up and down the ramp. If your shed uses clerestory windows for example to supplement or replace electrical lighting, remember that south-facing windows will provide the greatest amount of natural lighting.

Study the site plans shown in Figures 3-A to 3-D below for ideas concerning shed placement. If you create a site plan of your own, remember that it is essential to locate exterior doors and windows on your plan. Try to include all exterior structures and landscaping in your plan. While a scale drawing is not essential, it is not difficult to create a site plan to scale with a ruler and pencil. Grid paper with ¼" grids is perfect for drawing your preliminary site plan on a ¼"=1'-0" scale.

These site plans are provided for illustration purposes only. You should sketch your own site plan first and make certain that your proposed shed addition conforms to all applicable building codes before you begin construction. A little time devoted to planning before you begin will save time and money during the construction of your project.

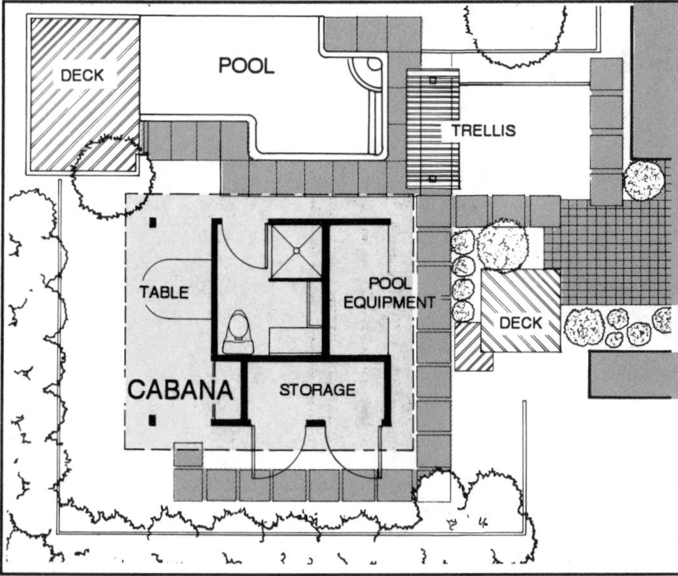

Figure 3-A

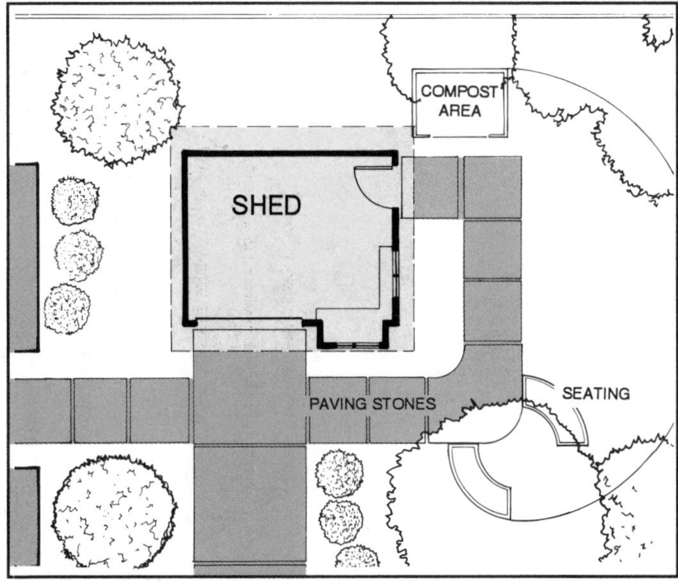

Figure 3-B

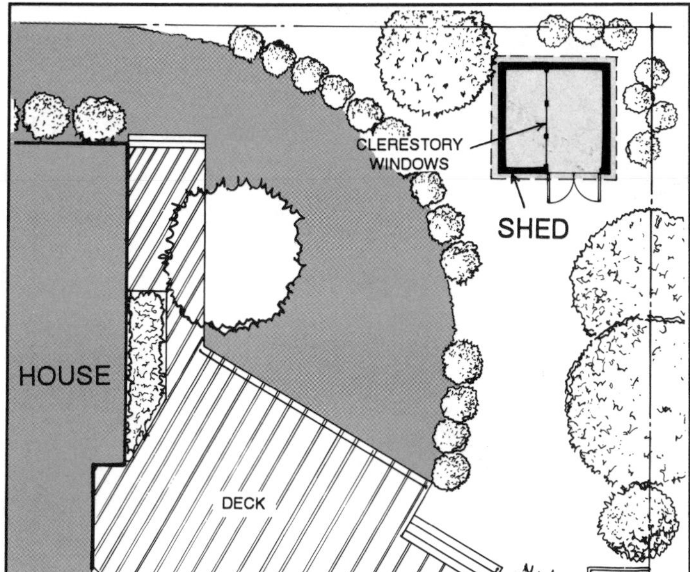

Figure 3-C

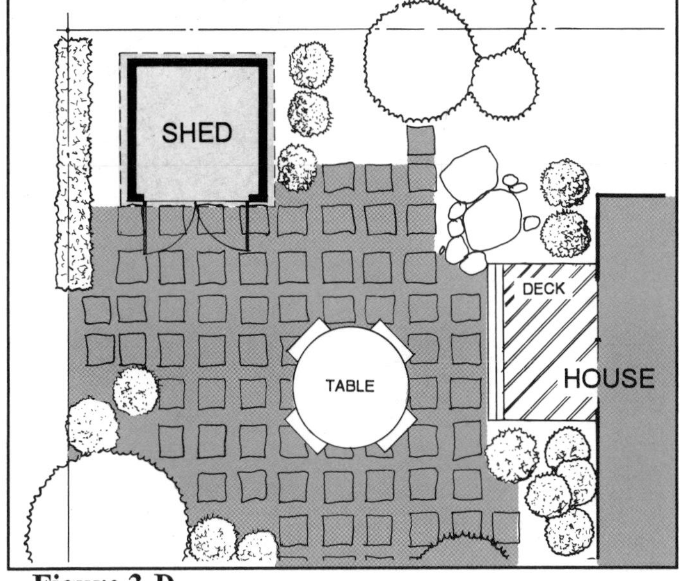

Figure 3-D

Typical Gable Roof Shed

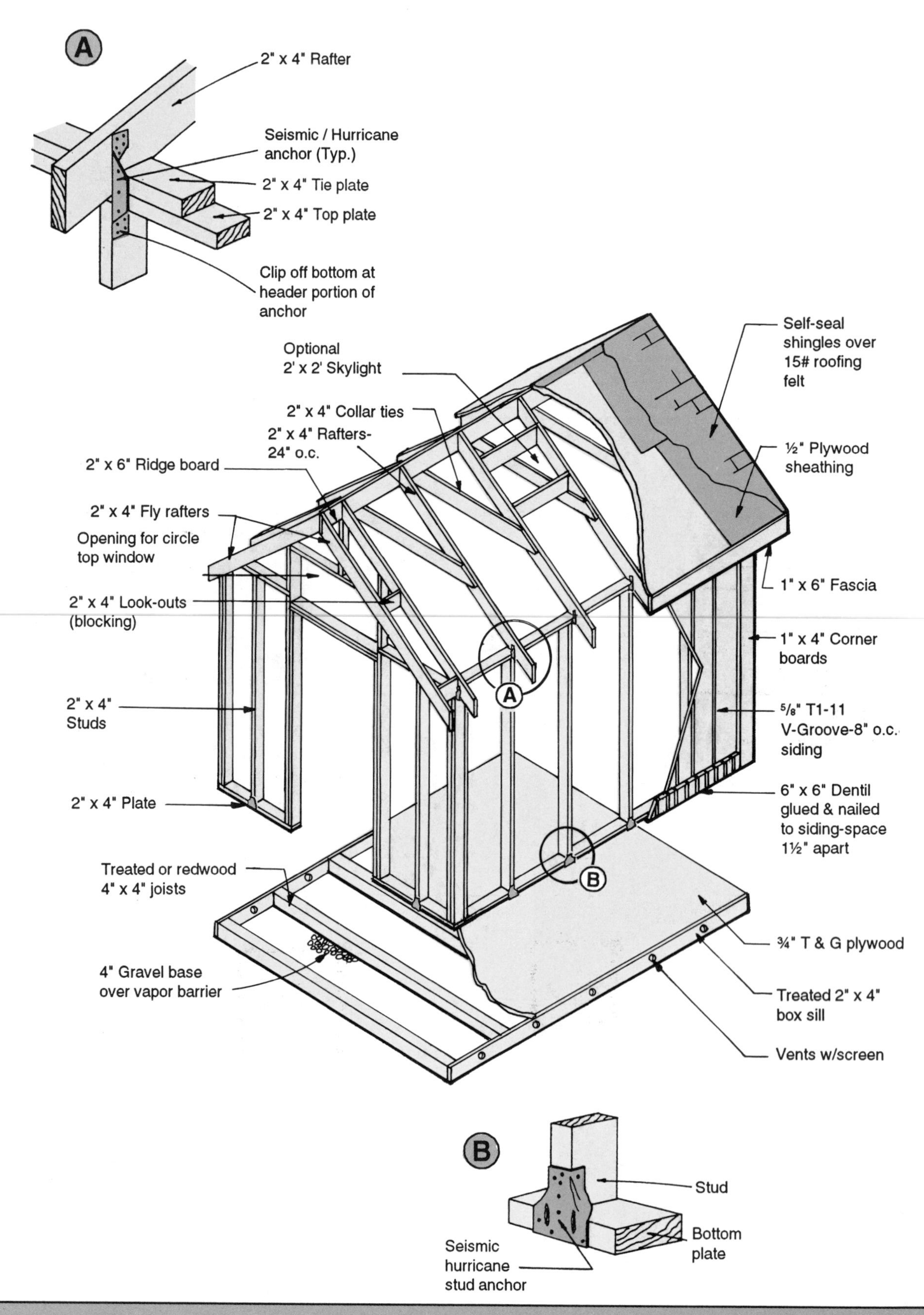

Typical Gambrel Roof Shed

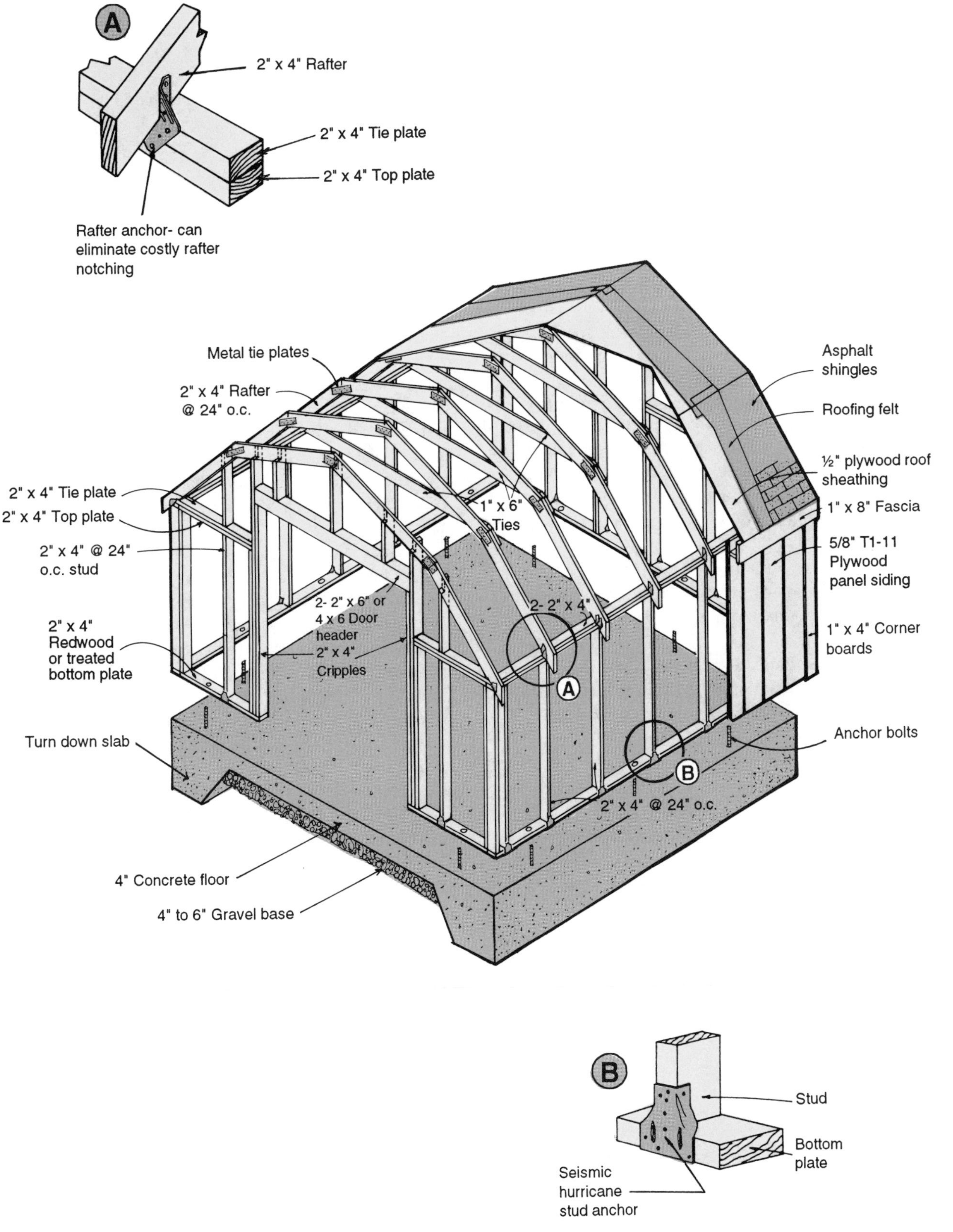

A

2" x 4" Rafter

2" x 4" Tie plate

2" x 4" Top plate

Rafter anchor- can eliminate costly rafter notching

Metal tie plates

2" x 4" Rafter @ 24" o.c.

2" x 4" Tie plate

2" x 4" Top plate

2" x 4" @ 24" o.c. stud

2" x 4" Redwood or treated bottom plate

Turn down slab

2- 2" x 6" or 4 x 6 Door header

2" x 4" Cripples

1" x 6" Ties

2- 2" x 4"

A

B

2" x 4" @ 24" o.c.

4" Concrete floor

4" to 6" Gravel base

Asphalt shingles

Roofing felt

½" plywood roof sheathing

1" x 8" Fascia

5/8" T1-11 Plywood panel siding

1" x 4" Corner boards

Anchor bolts

B

Stud

Bottom plate

Seismic hurricane stud anchor

Shed Glossary (A to M)

Anchor bolt. A metal connector device used to connect a wood mudsill to a concrete wall or slab.

Batterboards. Scrap lumber nailed horizontally to stakes driven near each corner of the foundation excavation. Stretch nylon strings between batterboards to transfer reference points and to measure elevation.

Beam. Beams are horizontal structural members that are supported by vertical posts. Beams are typically constructed from 2 or more 2-bys, 4-by material, or engineered lumber.

Bottom plate. In stud wall framing, the bottom horizontal member of the wall. Also known as the soleplate.

Bridging. Wood or metal cross pieces fastened between floor joists to provide structural strength and stability.

Cantilever. Refers to the end portion of a joist that extends beyond the beam.

Casing. Molding around door and window openings.

Codes. Regulations implemented by your local building department which control the design and construction of buildings and other structures such as sheds. Consult your local building department for applicable codes *before* you begin to build your shed.

Collar beam. A connecting member used between rafters to strengthen the roof structure.

Cornice. The structure created at the eave overhang which typically consists of fascia board, soffit, and moldings.

Cripple studs. Short studs that strengthen window and door openings or the gable end of a roof. Also known as jack studs.

Defect. Any defect in lumber whether as a result of a manufacturing imperfection or an irregularity in the timber from which the lumber was cut. Some defects are only blemishes while others can reduce strength and durability. Grading rules establish the extent and severity of wood defects.

Drip edge. Angled metal or wood located on the outer roof edge. Prevents water from running down the wall face.

Drywall. A gypsum panel used to finish interior walls. Also known as plasterboard or sheet rock.

Eave. The roof overhang projecting beyond the exterior wall.

Edge. The narrowest side of a piece of lumber which is perpendicular to both the face and the end.

Elevation. Drawing of a structure as it will appear from the front, rear, left and right sides.

Engineered lumber. Refers to beams or rafters constructed from wood fiber and glue such as glu-lams, micro-lams, or wood I-beams. Often superior in strength and durability to dimensional lumber.

Face. The widest side of a piece of lumber which is perpendicular to both the edge and the end.

Fascia. Trim used along the eave or gable end.

Finish. Any protective coating applied to your shed to protect against weathering. Shed finishes are available as stains, paints, or preservatives.

Flakeboard. A panel material made from compressed wood chips bonded with resin. Also known as oriented strand board (OSB) or chipboard.

Flashing. Metal material used on the roof, eaves, and butted wall panels to prevent moisture penetration.

Fly Rafters. Rafters at the gable end which "fly" unsupported by the tie plate. Also known as rake, barge, or verge rafters.

Footing. Concrete footings help to anchor your shed in the surrounding soil and distribute weight over a larger surface area. In climates where the soil freezes, a generous footing protects against soil heaves and structural slippage.

Frieze. A horizontal framing member that connects the siding with the soffit.

Frost Line. Measure of the maximum penetration of frost in the soil in a given geographic location. Depth of frost penetration varies with climate conditions.

Furring. Narrow strips of wood attached to walls or other surfaces that serve as a fastening base for drywall.

Gable. The triangular end of the roof structure formed by the roof framing.

Galvanized Nails. Hot-dipped galvanized nails (HDG) are dipped in zinc and will not rust.

Girder. Same as beam. A horizontal member that supports interior joists or walls.

Grade Stamp. A stamp imprinted on dimensional lumber which identifies wood species, grade, texture, moisture content, and usage. Grade descriptions such as select, finish, and common signify limiting characteristics that may occur in lumber in each grade. The stamp indicates a uniform measurement of performance that permits lumber of a given grade to be used for the same purpose, regardless of the manufacturer.

Grading. The process of excavating, leveling, and compacting the soil or gravel beneath your foundation to its desired finish level. Proper grading avoids drainage problems.

Grain. Lumber shows either a flat or vertical grain depending on how it was cut from the log. To minimize warping along the face of decking (known as cupping) and raising of the grain, you should place flat grain decking with the bark side up or facing out.

Header. A horizontal load-bearing support member over a door or window opening. Either double 2x or 4x material.

Heartwood. Core of the log that resists decay.

Hip rafter. A short rafter that forms the hip of a roof and runs from the corner of a wall to the ridge board. Usually set at a 45-degree angle to the walls.

Jack rafter. A short rafter that runs from the ridge board to a hip or valley rafter or from the hip rafter to the tie plate.

Joist. Typically 2-by lumber which is set on edge and supports a floor or ceiling. Joists in turn are supported by beams and posts. Floor joists can also be supported by wooden skids.

Joist hanger. A metal connector available in many sizes and styles that attaches to a ledger or rim joist and makes a secure butt joint between ledger and joist.

Lag Screw. Heavy-duty fastener with hexagonal bolt head that provides extra fastening power for critical structural connections. Use galvanized lag screws to prevent rust.

Ledger. A horizontal support member to which joists or other support members are attached.

Let-in brace. Usually a 1x4 corner brace in a wall section that runs diagonally from the bottom to top plate.

Look-out. Blocking which extends from an inner common rafter to the fly rafters at the gable ends.

Metal connectors. Used to augment or replace nails as

Shed Glossary (M to Z)

fasteners, metal connectors are critical for lasting and sturdy shed construction.

Moisture Content. Moisture content of wood is the weight of water in wood expressed as a percentage of the weight of wood from which all water has been removed. The drier the lumber the less the lumber will shrink and warp on your finished shed. Surfaced lumber with a moisture content of 19% or less is known as dry lumber and is typically grade stamped as "S-DRY." Moisture content over 19% results in a "S-GRN" stamp to indicate surfaced green. Avoid green lumber.

Mudsill. The part of the wall framing that contacts to the foundation. Should be pressure-treated to resist moisture and decay. Also known as the sill plate.

Outrigger. An extension of a rafter at the eave used to form a cornice or overhang on a roof.

Pea Gravel. Approximately ¼" round gravel material which can be used in a 4"-6" layer to cover the soil under your shed. Provides drainage and prevents soil-to-wood contact for sheds built on wooden skids rather than concrete foundation.

Perpendicular. At a 90 degree or right angle.

Pier. Piers support the total weight load of your shed and anchor the shed foundation to the soil. Concrete piers can either be precast in a pyramidal shape with a nailing block on top or poured in place. Precast piers are typically used in climates where the soil does not freeze hard. Poured in place piers are utilized where the soil freezes and must extend a certain depth below the frost line. Either precast or poured in place piers should have adequate footings to prevent movement of the pier in the soil. Consult your local building department for requirements regarding pier type and placement.

Pilot Hole. A slightly undersized hole drilled in lumber which prevents splitting of the wood when nailed.

Pitch. A measurement of roof slope. Expressed as the ratio of the total rise divided by the span.

Plumb. Absolutely vertical. Determined with either a plumb bob or spirit level.

Post. A vertical support member which bears the weight of the joists and beams. Typically posts are at least 4x4 lumber.

Pressure-Treated. Refers to the process of forcing preservative compounds into the fibre of the wood. Handle pressure-treated lumber with caution and do not inhale or burn its sawdust. Certain types of pressure-treated lumber are suitable for ground contact use while others must be used above ground. While more expensive than untreated lumber, pressure-treated wood resists decay and is recommended where naturally decay-resistant species like cedar or redwood are unavailable or too costly.

Purlin. A horizontal member of the roof framing that supports rafters or spanning between trusses.

Rafter. A roof framing member that extends from the top plate to the ridge board and supports the roof sheeting and roofing material.

Rake. The inclined end area of a gable roof.

Redwood. Decay-resistant and stable wood for exterior use. Heartwood grades provide the greatest decay resistance.

Reinforcing Bar. A steel rod which provides internal reinforcement for concrete piers and foundations. Also known as rebar.

Ridge board. A 1x or 2x member on edge at the roof's peak to which the rafters are connected.

Right Triangle, 6-8-10. A means of insuring squareness when you lay out your shed foundation. Mark a vertical line at exactly 8'-0" from the angle you want to square. Then mark a horizontal line at exactly 6'-0" from the crossing vertical line. Measure the distance diagonally between both the 6' and 8' marks and when the distance measures 10'-0" exactly you have squared a 90 degree angle between lines.

Rise. In roof construction the vertical distance the ridge rises above the top plate at the center of the span.

Rough sill. The lowest framing member of a door or window opening.

Scale. A system of representation in plan drawing where small dimensions represent an equivalent large dimension. In typical shed plans the drawings are said to be scaled down. Scale is expressed as an equation such as ¼"=1'-0".

Screed. A straight piece of lumber used to level wet concrete or the gravel under the foundation slab.

Sheathing. Exterior sheet (typically 4' x 8') material fastened to the rafters or exterior stud walls.

Skid. Typically a decay-resistant 4x4 member which is placed horizontally on the ground or gravel bed and which supports the shed flooring. Recommended use is only in dry climates with stable soil.

Slope. A measurement of ground inclination and expressed as a percentage of units of vertical rise per 100 units of horizontal distance.

Soffit. The underside of the roof overhang. Soffits can either be closed or open (thus exposing the roof rafters).

Span. The distance between structural supports such as bearing walls, columns, piers, or beams.

Spirit Level. A sealed cylinder with a transparent tube nearly filled with liquid forming a bubble used to indicate true vertical and horizontal alignment when the bubble is centered in the length of the tube.

String Level. A spirit level mounted in a frame with prongs at either end for hanging on a string. Determines level across string lines.

Stud. The vertical framing member of a wall.

T1-11 siding. Exterior siding material with usually 8" on center.

Tie plate. The framing member nailed to the top plates in order to connect and align wall sections. Also known as the cap plate or second top plate.

Toenail. To drive a nail at an angle. When you toenail a post to a beam for example, drive the nail so that one-half the nail is in each member.

Top plate. The horizontal top part of the wall framing perpendicular to the wall studs.

Tongue and Groove. Refers to the milling of lumber so that adjacent parts interlock for added strength and durability.

Trimmer stud. The stud adjacent to window or door opening studs which strengthens the opening and bears the weight of window or door headers.

Truss. A triangular prefabricated unit for supporting a roof load over a span. Trusses are relatively lightweight and can offer an easier method of roof construction for the novice.

Valley rafter. A rafter running from a tie plate at the corner of a wall along the roof valley and up to the ridge.

Choosing the Right Location

• Before you begin, consult with your local building department and obtain information regarding the placement, height, and square footage of outdoor storage buildings. For example, your local codes might specify that outbuildings cannot exceed a certain peak to ground height and that a shed must be offset a certain distance from property lines. If you disregard the code restrictions in your municipality, you will create problems for yourself and your neighbors. You might even be forced to remove a structure that violates local code requirements or to pay fines. If your local code requires a permit, submit a site plan and shed construction plans to your local building department and obtain all necessary permits ***before*** you begin construction.

• Remember that your shed will serve as an important storage addition to your home. With this goal in mind, be certain to select a location that will make shed access convenient but unobtrusive. Sketch a traffic plan that details major access paths in your yard and around your home to help you determine the correct location for your shed.

• Consider the building location in relationship to existing and future elements of your landscaping. Don't build a shed next to a tree whose growing roots will displace the shed foundation. Be certain that the placement of your shed in your backyard landscape matches the planned use of the shed. For example, if you want to use the shed in the winter, don't place the shed on the north side of a large evergreen tree which would completely block valuable winter sunlight.

• If at all possible, always select a well-drained location for your shed. A spot with poor drainage or soft ground will cause problems later on. Water accumulating under the shed creates condensation and can rust the materials you are storing inside.

Layout of the Shed Site

Accurately locating the four corners of the building will in turn establish the boundaries for the foundation. The site is laid out using batter boards set back from the corners of the planned building in an L-shaped arrangement. Setting the batter boards back from the actual building site allows you to maintain an accurate reference point as you dig footings and construct the foundation (See figure 8-A).

Batter boards are made of pointed stakes connected with 4' lengths of 1x4 lumber. Each batter board should form an accurate right angle when checked with a framing square. Batter board tops must be level with each other all the way around. Check for levelness with a string level or a mason's line level. Consult the step-by-step instructions on page 9 for help in establishing your site layout.

A variety of shed foundation construction methods are available depending upon your local site and your budget. If you do not want to anchor the shed permanently to one location, consider the wood skids and wood floor foundation detailed on page 10. Alternative foundation options are detailed on pages 11 and 12.

For example, in areas where the ground does not freeze during the winter, pier block foundations offer an inexpensive and sturdy method of anchoring your shed foundation. Pre-cast pier blocks with nailers are readily available at many building supply retailers and provide a relatively simple foundation base for the first time builder.

A more expensive and permanent alternative foundation is the turned-down or monolithic concrete slab. Concrete has the advantage of durability and resistance to moisture damage. If you do select a concrete slab, make sure that your slab will drain properly if moisture is released within your shed. Drainage for concrete slabs is especially important for cabana or greenhouse structures.

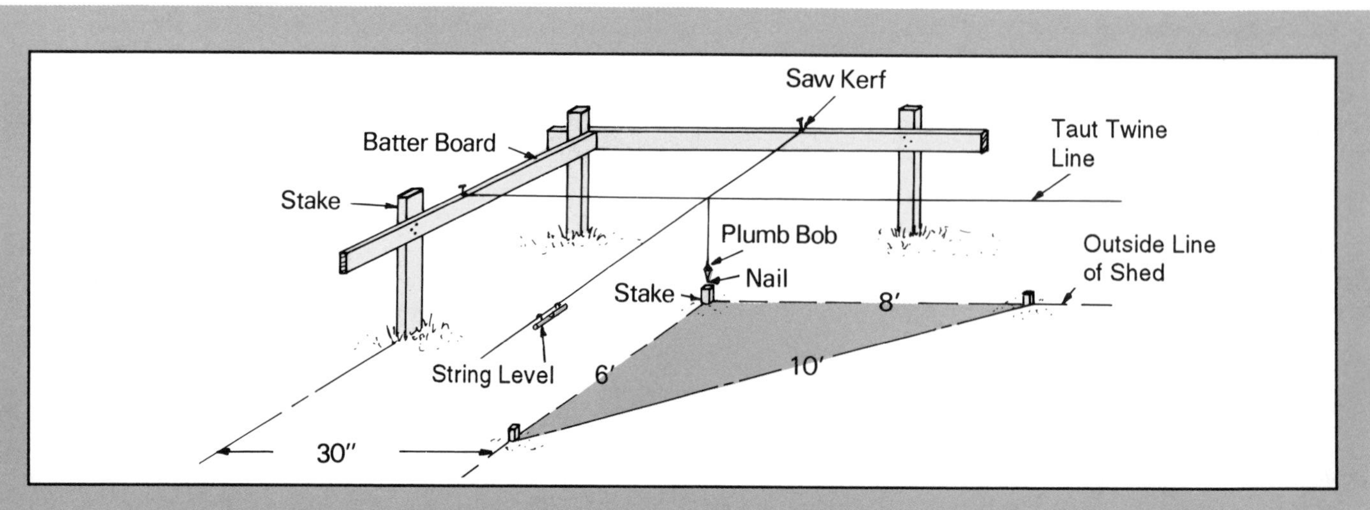

Figure 8-A Batter boards

Staking Out the Building

1. Accurately locate one corner of the building and drive stake **A** at that point (See figure 9-A).

2. Measure out along the long side of the building to the next corner. Drive in stake **B** at this point. Drive a small nail into the stakes and connect with tightly drawn twine.

3. Measure out the approximate positions of corners **C** and **D** and drive stakes at these points. Use a framing square to form an approximate right angle at these corners. Run twine from stakes **B** to **C**, **C** to **D**, and **D** to **A**.

4. You will now erect batter boards and adjust stake locations to form a true square or rectangular layout. Erect batter boards so that each corner stake is lined up directly on the diagonal from the opposite corner as illustrated. Use the line level to check that all batter boards are level with each other.

5. Stretch mason's twine between the batter boards so it is aligned directly over stakes **A** and **B**. When perfectly aligned make a saw kerf in the batter boards to make a permanent reference point and tack down the twine taut.

6. Stretch twine over stakes **B** and **C**. It must form a perfect right angle with twine **A-B**. Check for a perfect right angle using the **6-8-10 method**. Measure 6'-0" out along twine **A-B** and 8'-0" along twine **B-C**. Mark these points with pins. The diagonal between these two pins should measure exactly 10'-0". Adjust the position of twine **B-C** until the diagonal does equal 10'-0" and then notch the batter board at stake **C** and fasten off line **B-C**.

7. Using the **6-8-10 method** lay out twine **C-D** and **D-A**. At each corner carefully measure from the point where the twine lines cross each other to set building dimensions. Drop a plumb line at this intersecting point and set stakes in exact positions.

8. Check the final layout by measuring the diagonals between foundation stakes. The diagonals must be equal in length if your layout is squared up. If they are not, recheck your measurement and make proper adjustments.

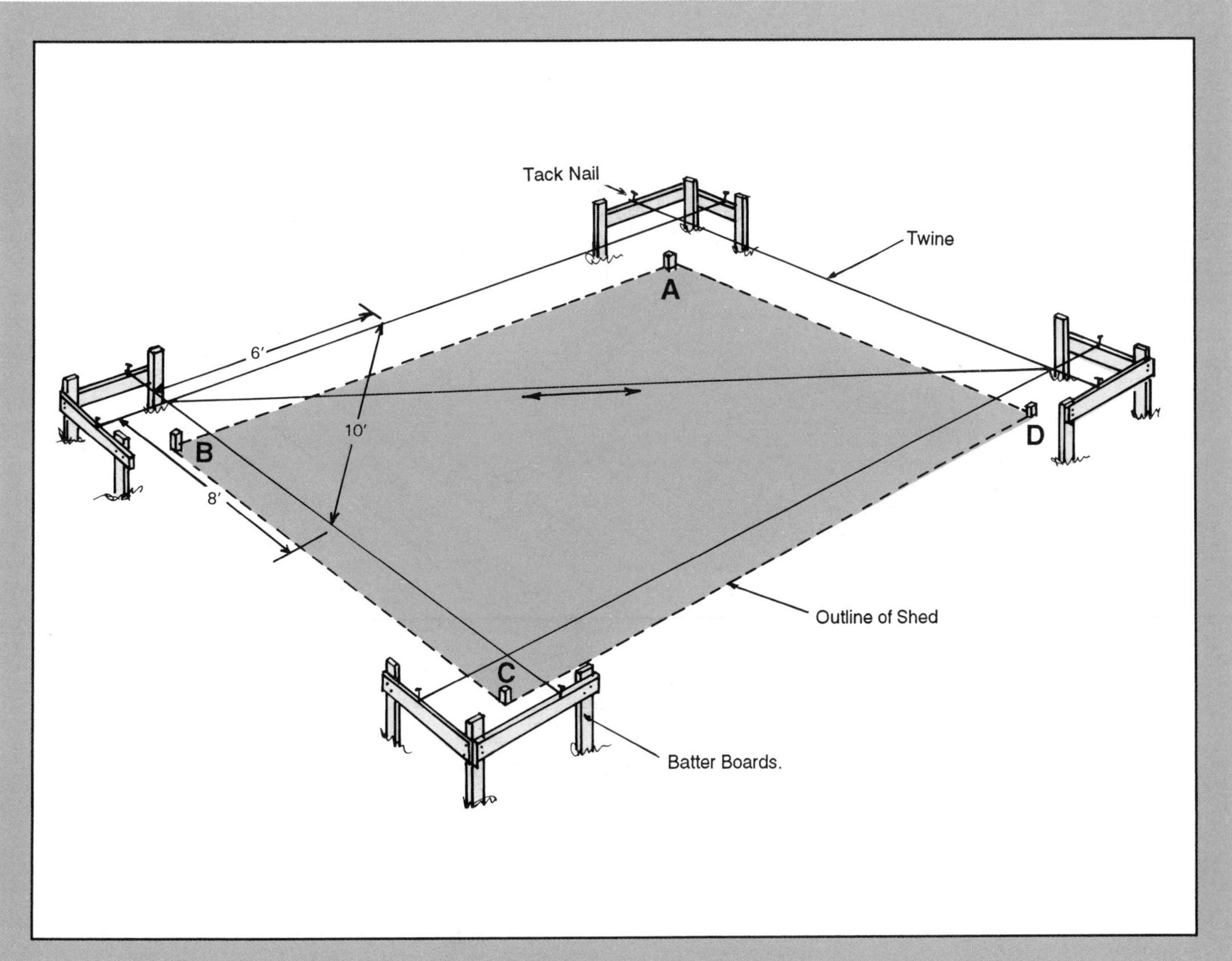

Figure 9-A Layout Procedure

Wood Skid and Wood Floor Foundation

1. Site Preparation. Prepare the site by scraping away all grass or weed material covering the shed area. If your soil does not drain well, remove 4"-6" of earth under the shed area and replace with 4" of pea gravel to increase drainage. Otherwise you can simply dig a drainage trench approximately 12" wide by 6" deep where the 4x6 skids are to be placed. Fill the drainage trench with gravel to ensure good drainage and to minimize the wood to soil contact.

2. Placing the skids. Skids should be either pressure-treated or redwood to prevent decay from ground contact. Position the 4x6 skids and make certain that the skids are level (See figure 10-A). Tie the skids together by nailing the outer 2x8 floor joist to the front and rear rim joist. Toe nail the outer joist to the skid. If you want to incline the shed floor slightly to ensure drainage, you should raise one end of both skids by an equal amount (1" for every 8' of skid) by placing additional gravel under the skid.

3. Constructing the Floor Frame. Having nailed the rim joist to the skids, you should now check that the floor frame is square. You can use the 6-8-10 method detailed on page 9 to ensure squareness. Complete the floor framing by adding the remaining 2x8 floor joists placed at 16" on center. Connect the floor joist to the rim joists with at least 3-16d coated sinkers at each end. If your budget allows it, use metal joist hangers to add extra strength to your floor joist framing.

4. Adding the Flooring. For extra strength and durability, use 4' x 8' x 3/4" Tongue and Groove exterior grade plywood for flooring. For normal use, install 4' x 8' x 3/4" CDX plywood to construct your floor. Fasten the floor framing to the floor joists using 8d nails 6" on center at the edge of the sheets and 10" on center along the intermediate floor joists. Take care to construct a stable and even floor which will serve as the foundation for your wall sections.

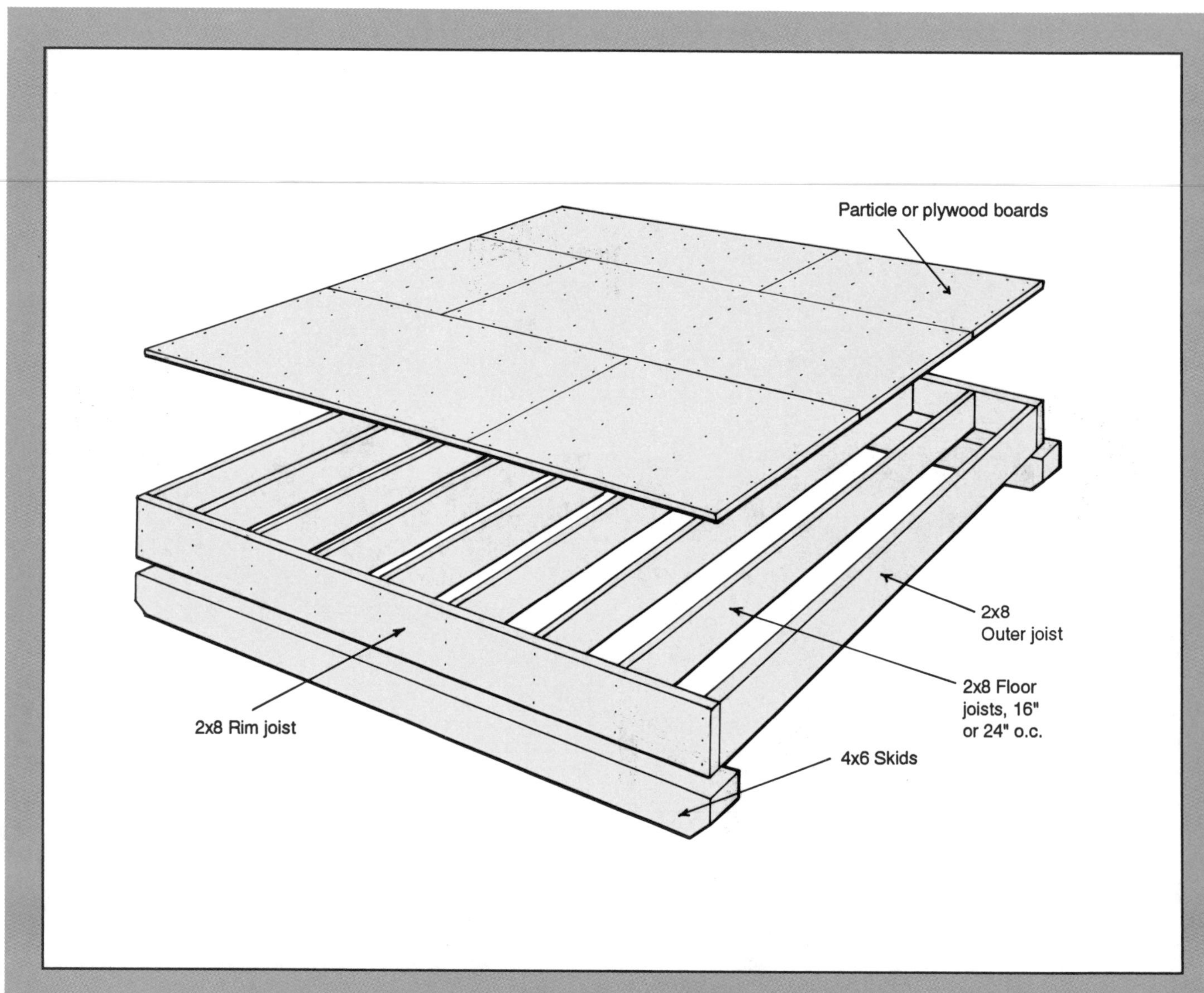

Figure 10-A Skid and Wood Floor Foundation

Concrete Pier and Wood Floor Foundation

1. Site Preparation. Prepare the site by scraping away all grass or weed material covering the shed area. If your soil does not drain well, remove 4-6" of earth and replace with 4" of pea gravel to increase drainage.

2. Locating the Piers. You will need to use your batter boards (see pages 8-9) to stretch a nylon string along the imaginary outer wall line. Use this string line to stake the pier locations at 4'-0" on center (See figure 11-A). The piers will support either a 4x6 beam or a built-up beam made from two 2x6's.

3. Pre-cast piers. If you are using precast concrete piers with an attached wooden nailer, you need to dig a pier footing at least 14" wide and 6" deep. The depth of the footing should be at least 6" below the local frost line. Pour the concrete into the footing hole. Spray the pier with water and then embed the pier at least 3" into the fresh concrete and twist slightly to achieve a solid bond between the concrete and the pier. Make certain that you have enough concrete in the hole so that the top of the nailer block is at least 4"-6" above grade level. Check the alignment of the pier by dropping a plumb bob from the centerline string. Finally, use a level across the block and tap the pier until it is level in all directions and square.

4. Attach the beam support posts to the piers. Cut 4x4 beam support posts to place the floor at a height above grade determined by local codes. If you don't require posts, simply toenail the 4x6 beam into the precast pier nailer blocks with 12d coated sinkers. If you require a certain grade to floor clearance, toe nail the posts into the nailer and then use a post cap connector to secure the beam to the post.

5. Constructing the floor framing and the floor. Follow the methods outlined in steps 3 and 4 on page 10 to construct the floor framing and the wood floor.

Optional Poured in-place Piers. First be certain you have purchased enough concrete to complete pier installation. Concrete is measured in cubic yards. To calculate the concrete required for a given number of cylindrical piers, use the following formula to find the **Total Volume in cubic yards:**

$$\text{Volume} = \frac{3.14 \times \text{Depth of Pier(Feet)} \times \text{Diameter (Feet)} \times \text{Diameter(Feet)} \times \text{No. Piers}}{108}$$

Example: Concrete required for twelve 10" diameter piers, 30" deep.

$$\text{Volume in cubic yards} = \frac{3.14 \times 2.5 \times .83 \times .83 \times 12}{108} = 0.61 \text{ Cubic Yards}$$

Remember to convert inches to feet (10 inches = .83 feet)
Conversion Factor: 27 Cubic Feet=1 Cubic Yard

Mix concrete according to manufacturer's instructions in a wheelbarrow or in a "half-bag" mixer. Use clean water for mixing and achieve the proper plastic consistency before you pour the concrete. If you are not using ready-mix concrete, prepare a **1:2:3 mix**--one part concrete, two parts river sand, and three parts gravel.

Coat the inside of the forms with oil to prevent sticking and dampen the inside of the hole with water before you pour the concrete.

With your post base anchors at hand, pour the concrete into the forms and tamp slightly to settle. For **poured in-place piers**, wait for the concrete to begin to harden and set the post base anchors into the concrete. Ensure that anchors are square and level. You can drop a plumb bob from your centerline string to be certain that your anchor is centered properly. Adjust post base anchors to the correct height.

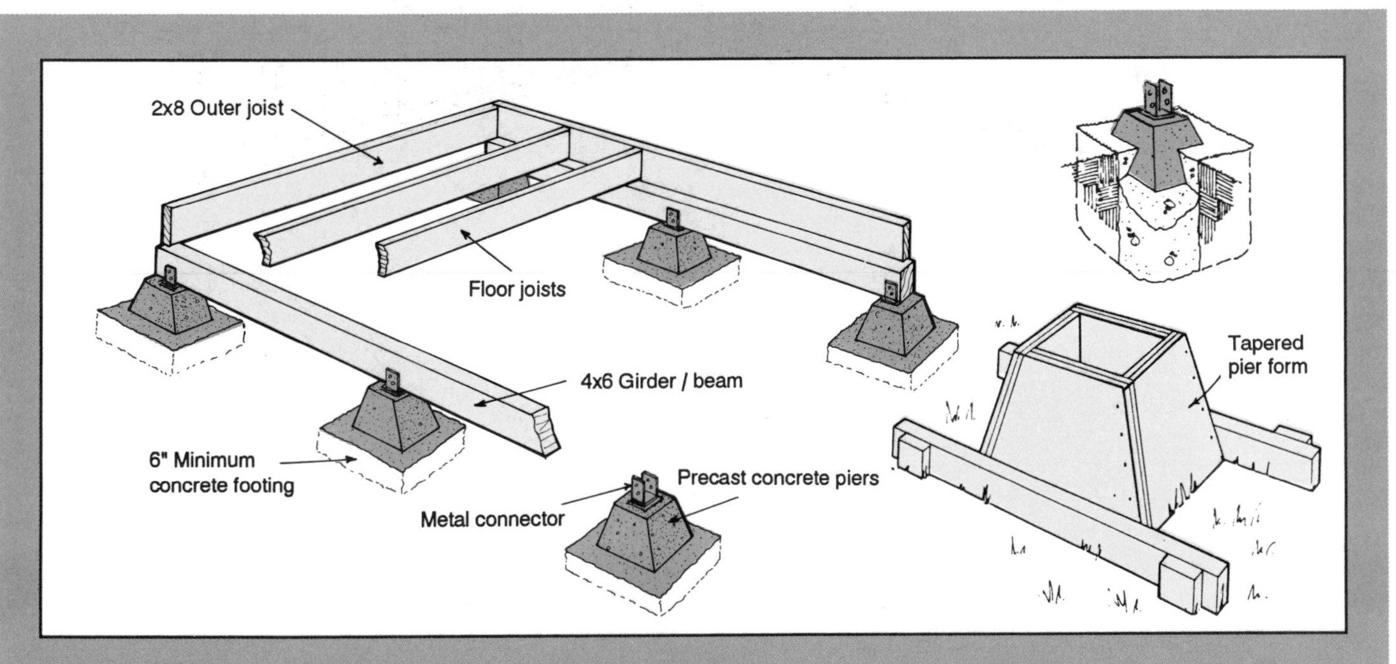

Figure 11-A Concrete Pier and Wood Floor Foundation

Concrete Slab Foundation

A concrete slab is the most permanent and durable method of constructing a foundation for your shed. However, slab construction requires greater preparation and expense than wood floor construction using skids or concrete piers.

1. Site Preparation. Prepare the site by scraping away all grass or weed material covering the shed area. Stake out the area for the slab. Be certain that all corners are square. If you are using a plan for slab construction, remember that all dimensions on the plan are to the outside of concrete. Excavate 4" of soil over shed area and replace with 4" of gravel to ensure proper drainage under slab. Level the gravel fill (See figure 12-A).

2. Digging the footing. Dig a trench for the slab footing approximately 8" wide at bottom and tapering inward to approximately 16" wide at top. The footing should extend down about 12" or at least 6" below the local frost line.

3. Building the forms. Use 2" scrap lumber to build the forms for the slab. Set the top of the 2" form board to the desired floor height and level. The inside face of form boards must line up exactly with "string lines" set at proper building dimensions. Brace your forms securely since you don't want them to shift or break when concrete is poured.

4. Preparing to pour the concrete. Place a 6 mil plastic vapor barrier over the gravel bed before you pour. Overlap the plastic sheets by at least 12" and do not puncture the plastic. If you want to insulate your slab from the earth, place 1" rigid foam insulation over the plastic provided that you have allowed for the additional height. Add two levels of ½" reinforcing bar (rebar) to the top and bottom of the footing and secure the rebar with tie wire held by nails in the forms. Finally place 6"x6" reinforcing wire mesh over the slab area and support the mesh with small wooden or masonry blocks so that it rests 2" above the vapor barrier.

5. Estimating the concrete. The following table will help you to estimate the approximate amount of concrete required to create a 4" thick slab with 18" deep footings.

Slab Size:	Concrete Required:
8' x 12'	2.5 cubic yards
12' x 12'	3.5 cubic yards
12' x 16'	5.0 cubic yards
12' x 20'	6.0 cubic yards

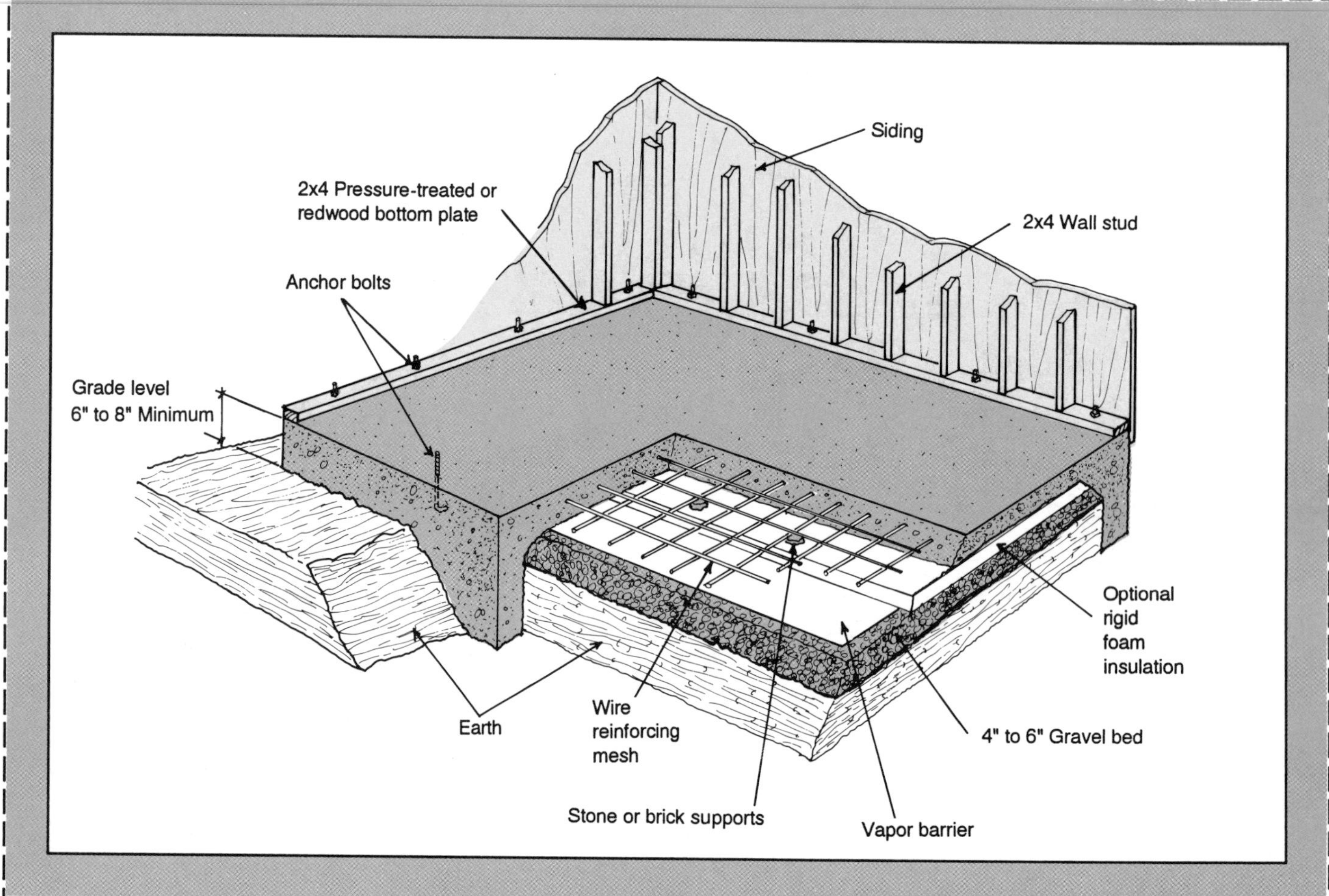

Figure 12-A Concrete Slab Foundation

Pouring the Concrete Slab

If necessary, have your local building inspector approve the forms before you pour. If your shed will utilize electrical service or plumbing, place the electrical conduit or plumbing in the proper location before you pour.

Placing

Be prepared for the arrival of the ready-mix truck or you could be charged a wait time fee. Have extra helpers, wheelbarrow, and concrete finishing tools at the ready. When the truck arrives, pour the area farthest from the truck and fill the footing trench making sure that the concrete does not push the forms or rebar out of alignment. For larger areas, break the work into smaller sections by installing temporary screeding guides.

When one section is poured move to the next section while the helpers screed off the first. Ask a helper to knock the sides of the forms with a hammer in order to force air pockets out of the concrete. Be sure that all voids are filled with concrete. Pay special attention to the perimeter area of the form boards. Remove the temporary screed guides when you fill in these voids.

Finishing

Once the concrete has lost its initial shine, begin finishing it with a bull float. Larger floats have a convenient handle like a broom. If you are using smaller hand floats, use toe and knee boards placed on the concrete so that you can kneel on the concrete without leaving a deep impression. Move the float in long sweeping motions.

Anchor bolts should be placed after the concrete has been screeded and bull floated. Place the bolts 1-3/4" away from the edge of the slab. Double-check bolt spacing and alignment.

For a coarser finish, bull floating is all that is required. For a slicker, smoother finish, use a steel trowel to go over the work once bull floating is complete. Use a light touch so you don't gouge the concrete surface. Before the concrete hardens completely, take a trowel and cut between the edge of the concrete and the form.

Curing

Once all finishing is completed, mist down the slab with water and cover it with a layer of plastic, burlap, or straw. Keep the surface moist for two to four days as the concrete cures.

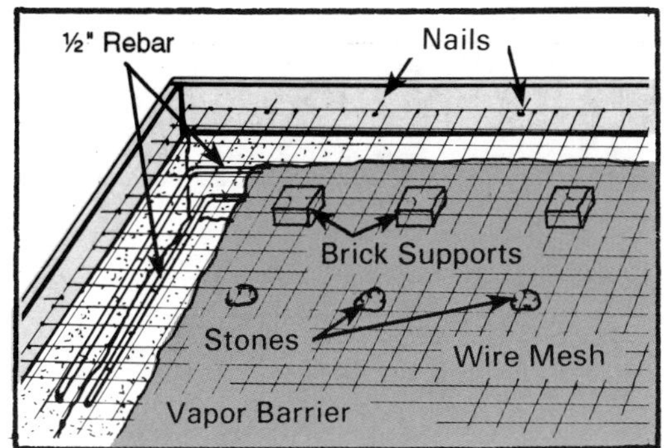

Steel reinforcing rods and wire mesh are laid into place over gravel and optional plastic vapor barrier.

Workers level concrete slab with a screed board.

Smooth concrete surface with a bull float.

Add anchor bolts.

Choosing Lumber for your Shed

The illustration below (see figure 14-A) will give you an idea of some of the defects found in dimensional lumber. Typical defects are **checks** that result from separation of wood across annual rings, **knots** that result from a portion of a tree branch incorporated in cut lumber, and **splits** which are a separation of the wood due to tearing apart of wood cells. A **shake** is a lengthwise separation of the wood which usually occurs between the rings of annual growth. None of the above defects should cause you to reject lumber outright. However, wood with a **bow, cup, crook, wane, split** or **twist** should be avoided in building construction.Dimensional lumber is typically sold in incremental lengths of 2 feet--for example, 2x6 lumber comes in lengths of 8,10,12,14,16,and 20 feet. When you plan your shed, you should try to consider standard board lengths in the overall dimensions of your shed. A 12'x16' shed (192 sq. ft.) will be far more economical to build than a shed measuring 11' x 19' (209 sq. ft.) due to wastage.

The chart below shows you how many studs to purchase for a given length of wall. You should add 2 studs for each corner and 2 extra studs for each door and window.

For example, a 2x6 board measures approximately 1-1/2" x 5-1/2" depending upon moisture content and surface. Lumber that has a **rough** surface will measure close to the nominal size in comparison to lumber that is surfaced on four sides (known as **S4S**).

The most critical factor in determining the actual sizes of dimensional lumber is the moisture content of the wood. Look for the grade stamp imprinted on lumber to determine moisture content. Typical moisture content ratings are:

- **MC 15** (less than 15% moisture content)
- **S-DRY** (less than 19% moisture content)
- **S-GRN** (greater than 19% moisture content)

A 2x6 surfaced unseasoned board (S-GRN) will actually measure 1 9/16" x 5 5/8" compared to 1 1/2" x 5 1/2" for a 2x6 rated surfaced dry (S-DRY). The chart below shows actual versus nominal sizes of dimensional lumber which is S4S and S-DRY or better. Avoid unseasoned lumber especially in the framing of your shed. Lumber which is unseasoned can shrink considerably as it dries naturally and is certain to cause structural problems as your shed ages.

Studs Required for walls:	Wall Length in Feet: 2	3	4	5	6	8	9	10	11	12	14	16	20
16" on center	3	3	4	5	6	6	7	8	9	9	12	13	16
24" on center	2	3	3	4	4	5	5	6	7	7	8	9	11

STANDARD DIMENSIONS OF SURFACED LUMBER	
Nominal size	Surfaced (actual) size
1 × 2	3/4" × 1-1/2"
1 × 3	3/4" × 2-1/2"
1 × 4	3/4" × 3-1/2"
1 × 6	3/4" × 5-1/2"
1 × 8	3/4" × 7-1/4"
1 × 10	3/4" × 9-1/4"
1 × 12	3/4" × 11-1/4"
2 × 3	1-1/2" × 2-1/2"
2 × 4	1-1/2" × 3-1/2"
2 × 6	1-1/2" × 5-1/2"
2 × 8	1-1/2" × 7-1/4"
2 × 10	1-1/2" × 9-1/4"
2 × 12	1-1/2" × 11-1/4"
4 × 4	3-1/2" × 3-1/2"
4 × 10	3-1/2" × 9-1/4"
6 × 8	5-1/2" × 7-1/2"

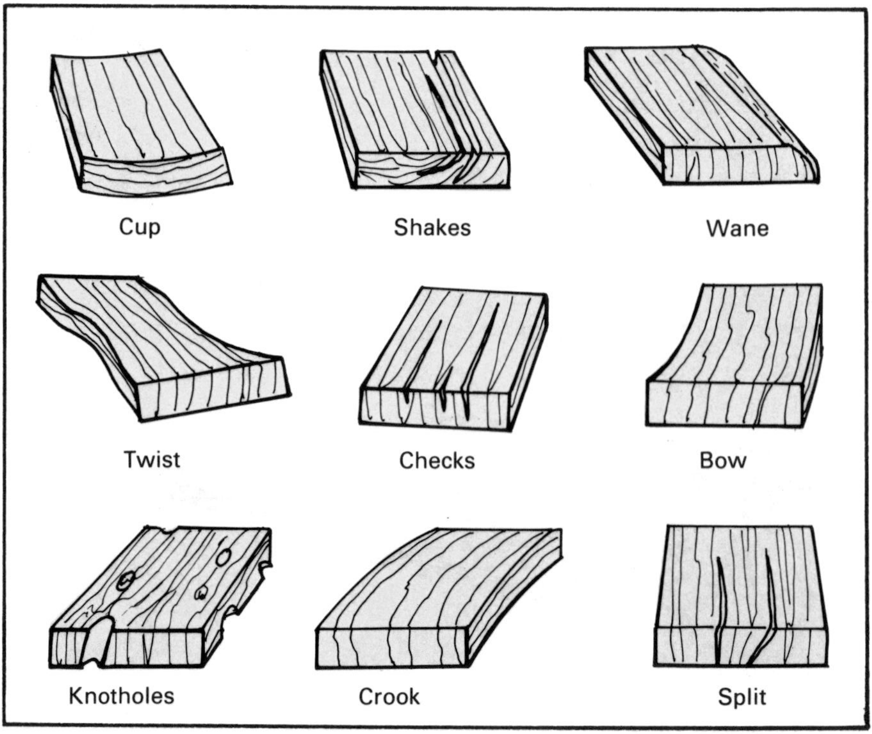

Figure 14-A Lumber Defects

Choosing Lumber for Your Shed

Choosing the correct lumber for your shed can be as consequential as determining the correct design. For use in a shed, the lumber you select must perform well in an exposed outdoor environment. Performance is measured according to the following criteria:

· **Freedom from Shrinkage and Warping.** Lumber which has dimensional stability will not cause problems later.

· **Decay Resistance.** Generally lumber cut from the heartwood (center of the log) is more resistant to decay than lumber cut from sapwood (outside of the log). However, chemical pressure-treatment can provide decay resistance to species which lack this property.

· **Workability.** Refers to the ease with which you can saw, nail, or shape lumber.

· **Nail Holding.** Determines whether or not a given species possesses good nail-holding power.

· **Paint Holding.** The ability to hold a finish. Some species which contain high levels of natural extractives (such as pitch or resins) do not hold a finish well.

· **Fire Resistance.** All woods are combustible, but some resist fire better than others. Woods which do not contain large amounts of resin are relatively slow to ignite.

· **Strength and Weight.** Wood which is relatively light in weight but possesses great strength is ideal.

While no single species performs ideally according to all of the criteria above, your local lumber dealer will be able to advise you regarding the lumber species most suited to your area. Often you must balance considerations of economy with performance. For example, redwood is considered a premium construction material, but high transportation costs outside the area of manufacture make pressure-treated pine woods a more economical alternative.

Here is a concise guide to some common softwood lumber species used in shed construction:

· **Cedar, Western Red.** Popular for the durability and decay-resistance of its heartwood.

· **Cypress.** Cypress resists decay, has an attractive reddish coloration, and holds paint well.

· **Douglas Fir, Larch.** Douglas fir has great strength and is used best in the framing of your shed, especially in the floor joist members.

· **Pines.** Numerous pine species have excellent workability but are often pressure-treated for use in exterior construction.

· **Southern Pine.** Unlike the soft pines described above, southern pines possess strength but are only moderately decay and warp resistant.

· **Poplar.** Has moderate strength, resists decay and warping.

· **Redwood.** A premium construction material because of its durability, resistance to decay, and beautiful natural brownish-red coloration.

Remember that in certain circumstances you can use two different species of lumber to construct your shed. For example, redwood can be used for exterior trim while douglas fir is used for strength in the shed wall and roof framing.

Whatever lumber species you select, it is important to learn the difference between the grain patterns in dimensional lumber. **Flat grain** lumber is cut with the grain parallel to the face of the board. Typically used for decking, flat grain boards should be used with the bark-side up in order to minimize cupping and grain separation. **Vertical grain** lumber, a more expensive grade used for finish work, is cut with the grain perpendicular to the face of the board.

Using Engineered Lumber

Due to recent developments in timber cutting practices and the reduced availability of certain sizes of framing lumber, engineered lumber manufactured from plywood, wood chips, and special glue resins offers an attractive alternative to dimensional lumber used for joists, beams, headers, and rafters. Unlike sawn dimensional lumber, engineered lumber is a manufactured product that will not warp and shrink over time.

Engineered lumber is manufactured to meet stringent criteria for strength, uniformity, and reliability. **Glu-lam beams** offer great strength over spans. **Wood I-beams** provide a lightweight alternative to conventional rafters. Some typical **laminated veneer lumber** products are shown to the right.

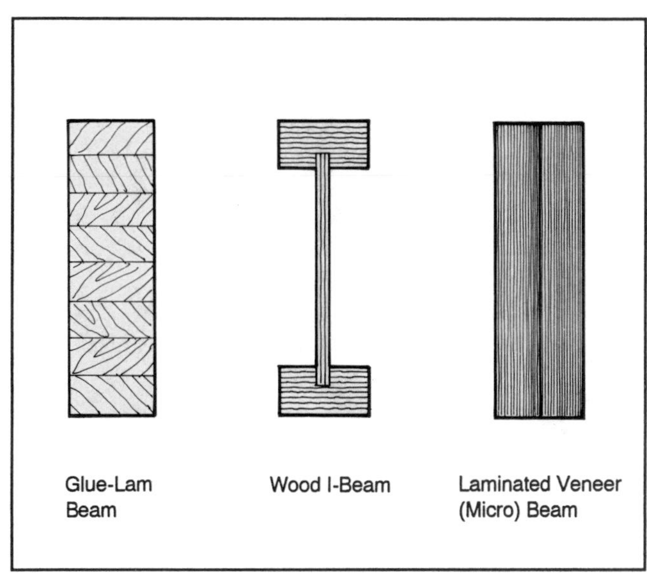

Ordering Shed Materials

Complete the sample material list below before you begin to shop. If you are using one of the shed plans offered in the back of this manual, each plan comes with a complete bill of materials. If you have designed your own shed, create a material list from the final design after approval by your local building department.

Once you have completed the sample material list, you should visit several reputable building supply dealers to shop for your materials. Be aware that you will add to the cost of your project if you purchase your materials in a piecemeal fashion. Obtain competitive bids on your bill of materials from different dealers. Keep in mind that the quality of materials and the level of service provided by the dealer are hidden factors in selecting your supplier. Some dealers will offer you a low price but will not provide free on-site delivery. Delivery charges can more than offset a low initial bid.

Especially consider the quality and grade of the lumber you are purchasing. Poor quality materials will yield a meager return on your shed investment.

Don't hesitate to order at least a 5-10% overage of materials to make up for inevitable cutting mistakes or lumber defects. Be aware that dimensional lumber is sold either by the board foot, the lineal (or running) foot, or by the piece. A board foot of lumber represents the amount of lumber in a board 1" thick x 12" wide x 12" long. Use the following formula to compute board feet:

$$\text{Board Feet} = \frac{\text{Length(Feet)} \times \text{Width(Inches)} \times \text{Thickness(Inches)}}{12}$$

Sample Materials List

	SIZE	LENGTH	QUANTITY X	COST =	TOTAL COST
FOUNDATION					
Concrete					
Sand					
Gravel					
SUBSTRUCTURE					
Girders					
Skids					
Floor Joists					
Rim Joists					
4'x8'-3/4" CDX Plywood					
WALL FRAMING					
Bottom Plates					
Cripple Studs					
Wall Studs					
Top and Tie Plates					
Headers over Doors					
Headers over Windows					
ROOFING & SIDING					
Rafters					
Collar Ties					
Fly Rafters					
Ridge Board					
4'x8'-1/2" Roof Sheathing					
Roofing Felt					
Self-sealing Shingles					
4'x8'-1/2" T1-11 Siding					
WINDOWS & DOORS					
Windows					
Doors					
CONNECTORS					
Nails					
Screws					
Bottom plate to stud ties					
Tie plate to rafter ties					
GRAND TOTAL					

Nails and Fasteners for Shed Construction

Nails are the most common fastener used in shed framing and construction. Nail lengths are indicated by the term penny, noted by a small letter **d.** In most cases, nails increase in diameter as they increase in length. Heavier construction framing is accomplished with common nails. The extra thick shank of the common nail has greater strength than other types. A wide thick head spreads the load and resists pull-through. For the substructure and framing of your shed where nails are hidden, consider vinyl coated sinkers or cement coated nails which bond to the wood and will not pull up as readily as uncoated nails.

Box nails are similar in shape to common nails, but they have a slimmer shank that is less likely to split wood. Finishing nails are used in work where you want to counter sink and then cover the nail head.

Roofing nails are essential for attaching roofing materials and preventing moisture penetration through the nail hole.

Screws create neat, strong joints for finished work. Heavy-duty **lag screws** and **lag bolts** are useful for heavier framing connections, such as girder-to-post.

Discuss your project with your local hardware or building supply dealer to determine the best nail and fastener selections for your shed project.

FINISHING NAIL SELECTION CHART

SIZE	LENGTH	GAUGE	APP. # PER LB.
10d	3"	11½	120
8d	2½"	12½	190
6d	2"	13	310
4d	1½"	15	600
3d	1¼"	15½	870
2d	1"	16	1000

TABLE OF COMMON NAILS

SIZE	LENGTH	GAUGE	#PER LB.
2d	1"	15	840
3d	1¼"	14	540
4d	1½"	12½	290
5d	1¾"	12½	250
6d	1"	11½	160
7d	2¼	11½	150
8d	2½"	10¼	100
9d	2¾"	10¼	90
10d	3"	9	65
12d	3¼"	9	60
16d	3½"	8	45
20d	4"	6	30
30d	4½"	5	20
40d	5"	4	16
50d	5½"	3	12
60d	6"	2	10

This table of common nails shows the approximate number of nails you get in a pound. You'll need more pounds of larger sizes to do a job. For outside jobs, get galvanized or cadmium-plated nails. Aluminum nails are a bit expensive unless you're doing a small project.

Common Types of Fasteners

Common Nail
Box Nail
Finishing Nail
Casing Nail
Vinyl-Coated Sinker
Roofing Nail
Lag Screw
Machine Bolt
Carriage Bolt
Spiral Nail
Annular Ring Nail
Metal Anchor
Washer
Nut

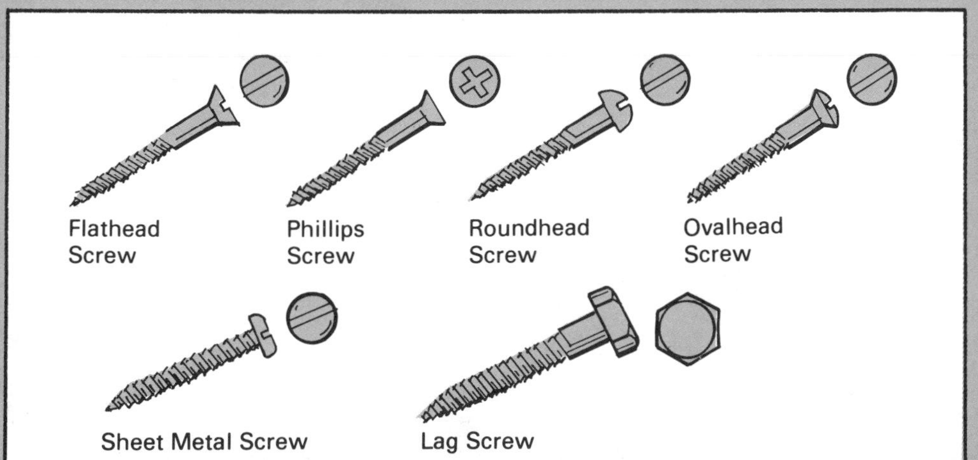

SCREW SELECTION CHART

Size	Length	Size	Length
0	1/4-3/8	9	1/2-3
1	1/4-1/2	10	1/2-31/2
2	1/4-3/4	11	5/8-31/2
3	1/4-1	12	5/8-4
4	1/4-11/2	14	3/4-5
5	3/8-11/2	16	1-5
6	3/8-21/2	18	11/4-5
7	3/8-21/2	20	11/2-5
8	3/8-3	24	3-5

This chart shows sizes and the lengths in which they're available. The larger sizes come in longer lengths. Most jobs call for sizes 6 to 12 in ½ to 3 inch lengths. Check size and length before you buy.

Framing with Metal Fasteners

A wide variety of metal fasteners are available to make your shed sturdy and long-lasting. You may be required by local codes to add **seismic and hurricane connectors** to each stud where it connects to the bottom and top plate. **Rafter and tie plate connectors** offer a quick method of attaching the roof rafters to the tie plate *without* making a bird's mouth cut. **Nail-on plates** can replace plywood gussets in gambrel roof construction and help to create a rigid roof frame. Be sure to follow the manufacturer's installation instructions.

Right-angled **corner framing anchors** add strength to perpendicular butt joints, especially where rim joists meet. Use **joist hangers** to attach your floor joists to rim joist members. **Beam connectors** provide a strong connection between beams and posts or pier blocks. The modest additional expense of metal fasteners will be more than offset by the added durability of your shed. Secure fasteners using the short ribbed nails provided or where extra strength is required use lag screws in addition to nails.

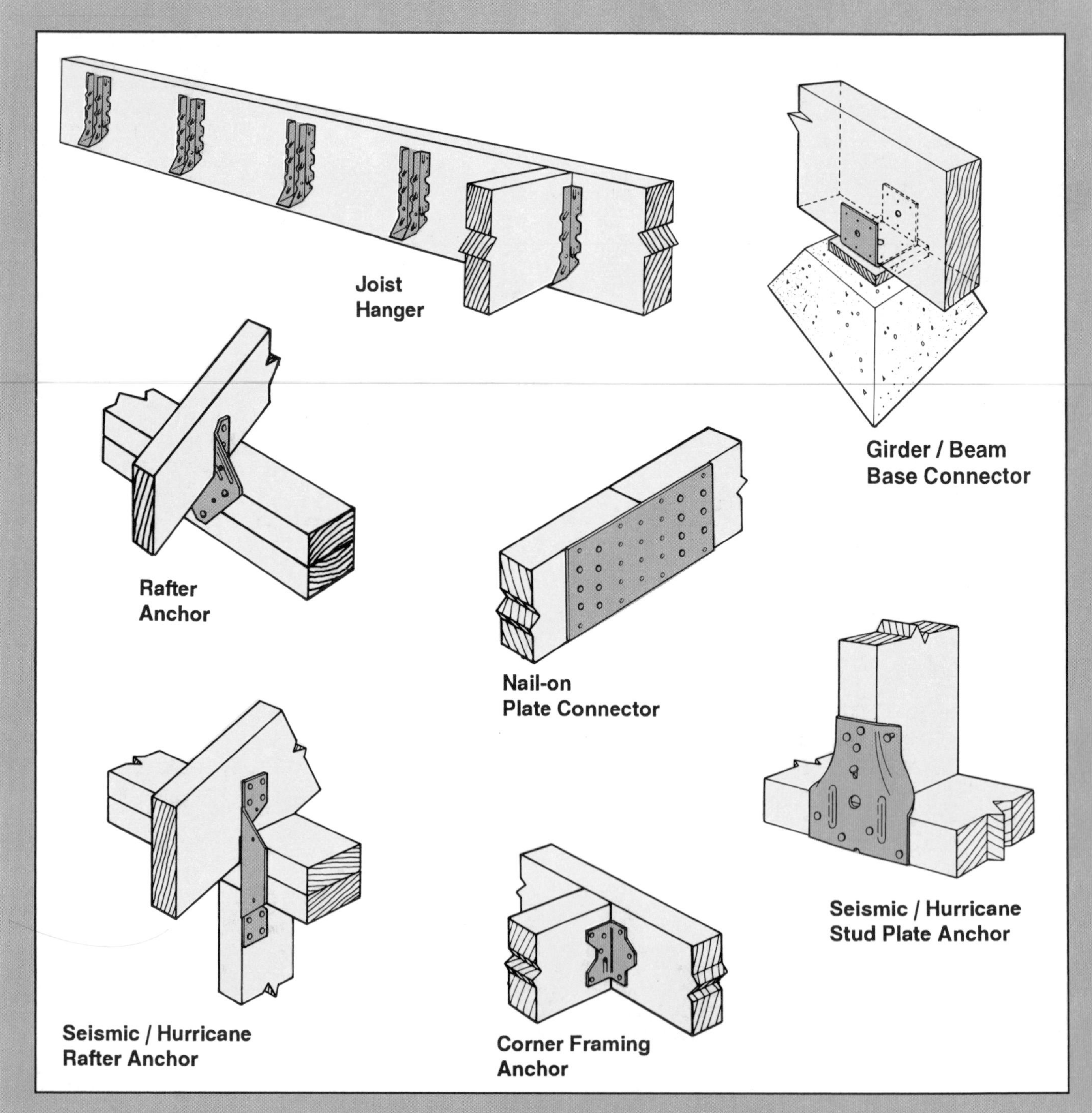

Illustrations courtesy of Simpson Strong-Tie Co., Inc.

Framing with Metal Fasteners (Continued)

Girder / Beam Frame Connector

Available sizes for:
2 x 4 Joists
2 x 6 Joists

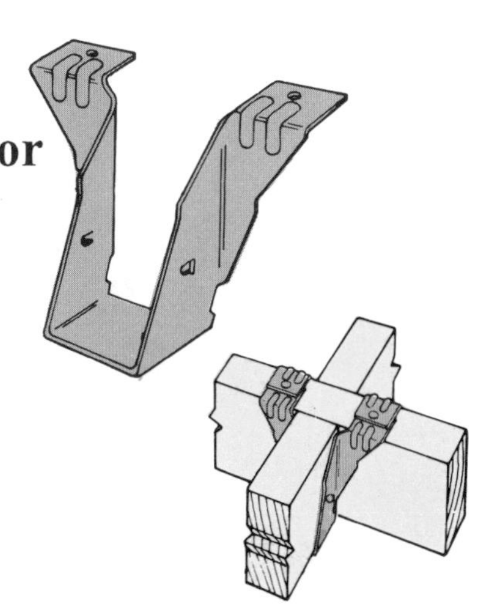

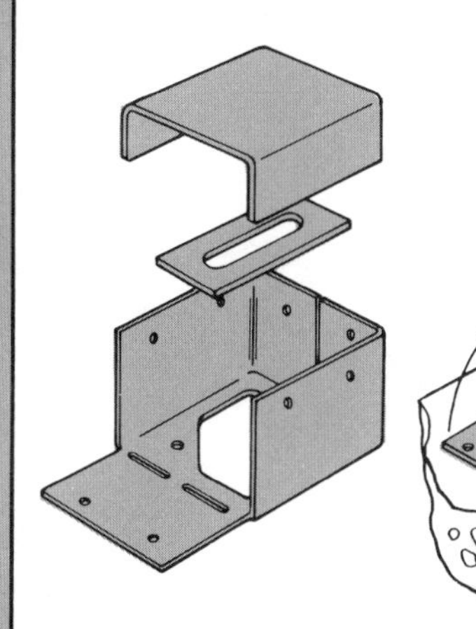

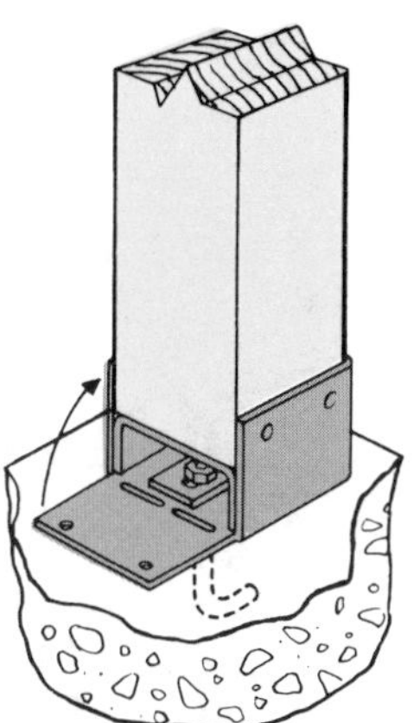

Adjustable Post Anchor

Available sizes for:
4 x 4 Posts
4 x 6 Posts
6 x 6 Posts

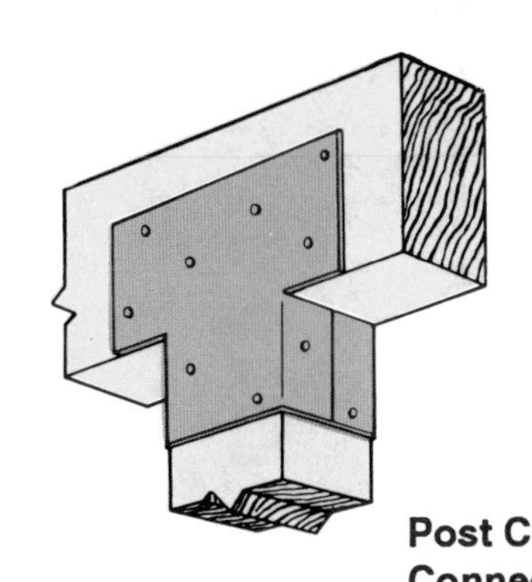

Post Cap Connector

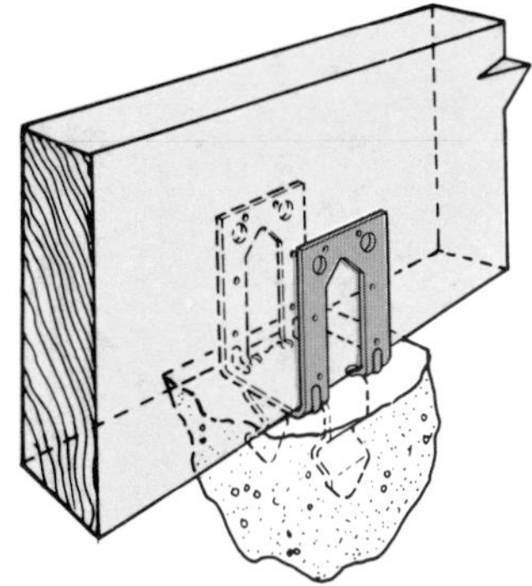

Girder / Beam Base Connector

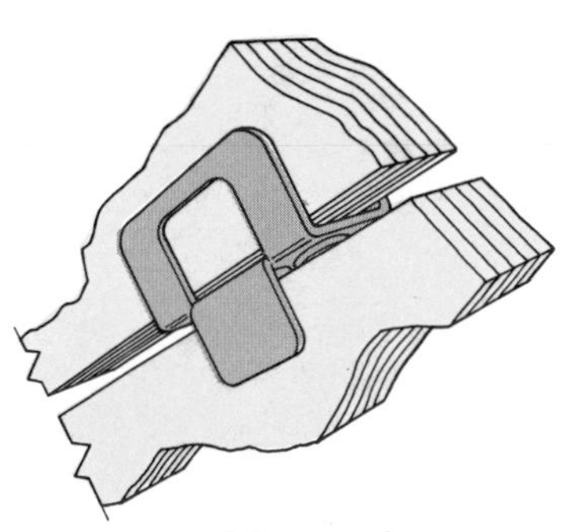

Plywood Sheathing Clips

Typical Shed Floor Plan

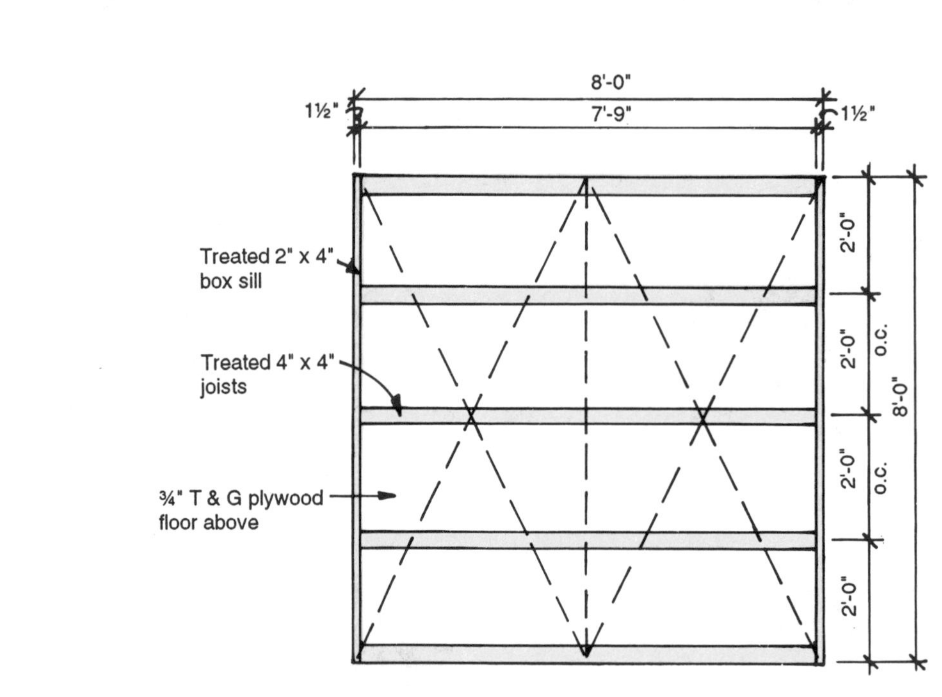

FLOOR FRAMING PLAN

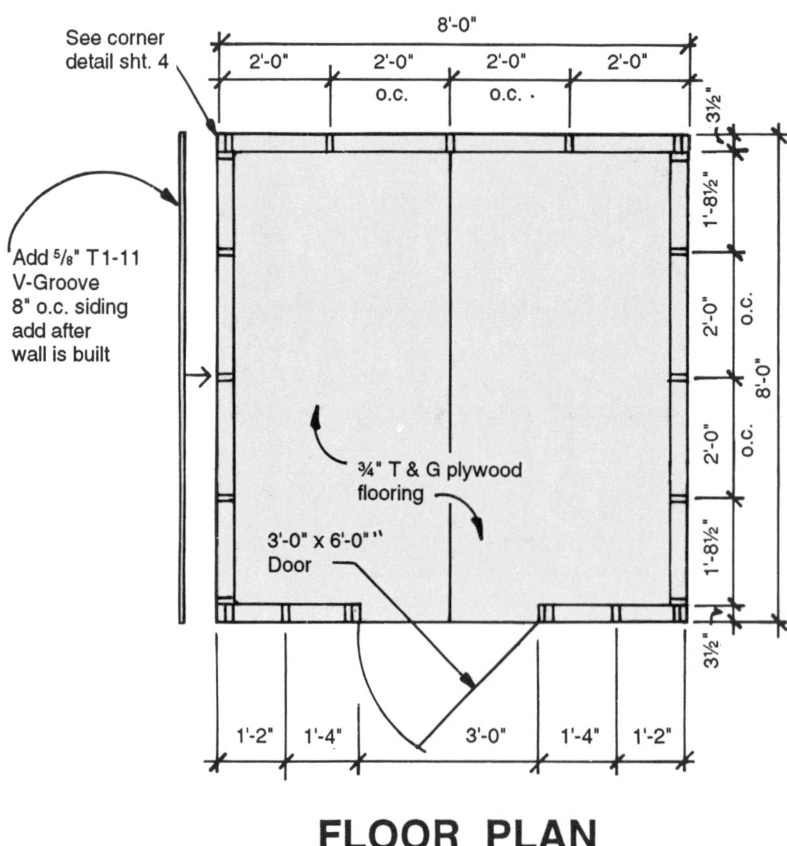

FLOOR PLAN

Typical Shed Wall and Roof Framing Plan

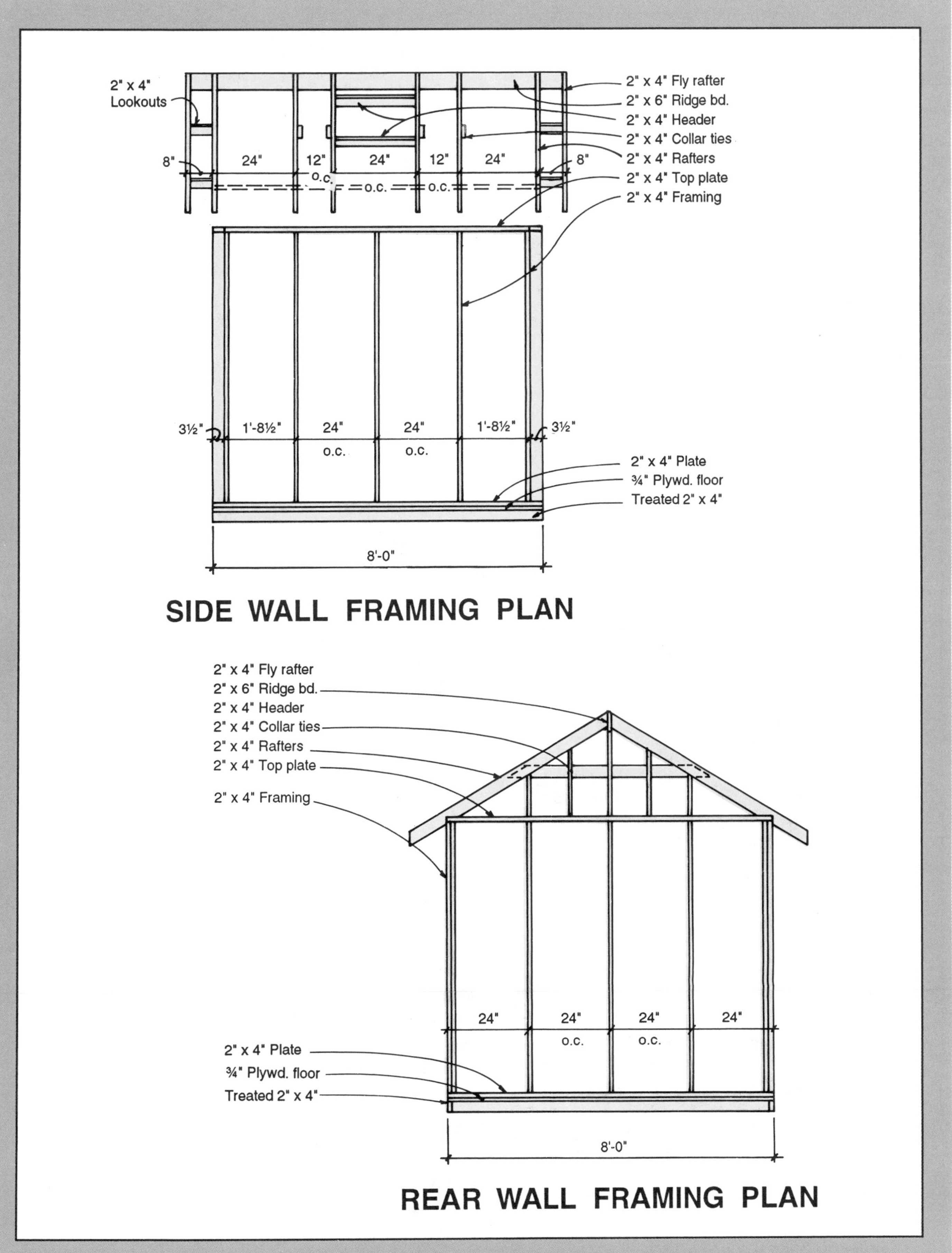

Constructing the Basic Wall Frame

To begin, cut both the top and bottom plates to length. In most cases, you will need more than one piece of lumber for each plate. So locate the joints at stud centers and offset joints between top and bottom plates by at least 4'-0" (See figure 22-A).

Lay the top plate against the bottom plate on the floor as illustrated below. Beginning at one end, measure 15-¼" in and draw a line across both plates. Measure out farther along the plates an additional distance of 1-½" from this line, and draw a second line. The first interior stud will be placed between these lines. From these lines, advance 16" at a time, drawing new lines, until you reach the far end of the plates. Each set of lines will outline the placement of a stud with all studs evenly spaced at 16" on center. If you are using studs on 24" centers, the first measurement in from the edge would be 23-¼".

Assembling the Pieces

If you are using **precut studs** (either 92-¼" or 92-⅝" in length), no cutting is required. Otherwise measure and cut the wall studs to exact length. Position the plates apart on the floor and turn them on edge with the stud marking toward the center. Place the studs between the lines and nail them through each plate with two 16d common nails.

Framing Corners

Where walls meet, you might need extra studs to handle the corner tie to the adjacent wall. These extra studs should be added to the ends of the longer two of the four walls. The exact positioning of these extra corner studs is shown at the bottom of page 26.

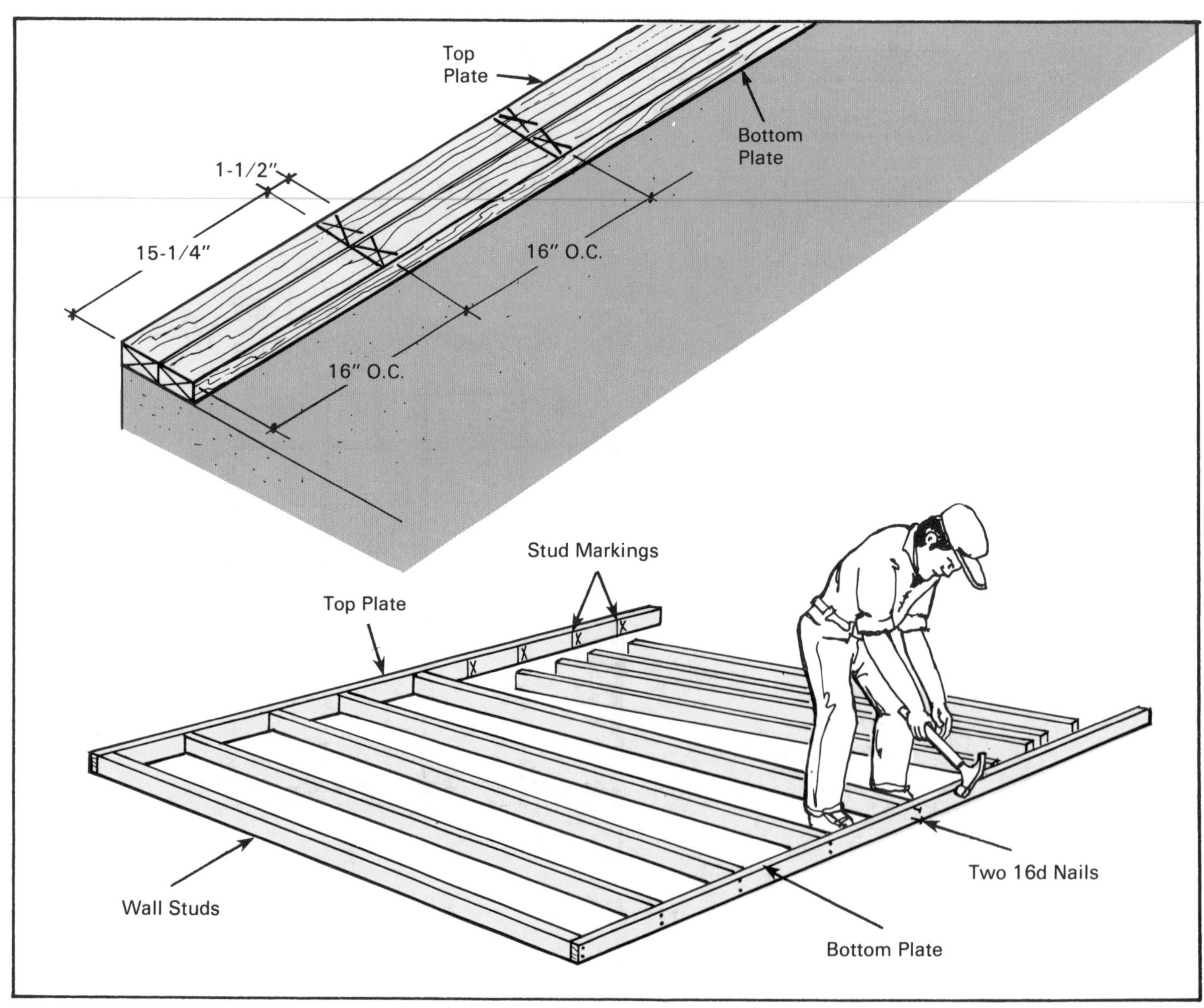

Figure 22-A Assembling the Wall Frame

Door and Window Framing

At door and window openings there is no stud support, so a header is required. Door and window headers can be constructed either from 4x dimensional lumber, veneer laminate lumber also known as engineered lumber, or two lengths of 2x material on edge with a ½" piece of plywood sandwiched between them. When you are constructing a built-up header from doubled-up 2by material, the plywood makes the header the same 3-½" width as the studs.

Headers are always installed on edge as shown. Consult the chart at right to determine the header size required for a given span.

The spaces above door openings and above and below windows are framed with cripple studs spaced 16" on center. Study the illustrations to become familiar with the king and trimmer stud locations used in framing doors and windows.

The rough framed door should be 1-½" higher than the usual 80" actual door height and 2-½" wider than the door to account for doorjamb material. When the 1-½" bottom plate is cut from the opening, this adds the needed 1-½" in extra height.

In addition to cripple studs, king studs, and trimmer studs, window framing also uses a rough sill to support the window. Headers should be set at the same time as door headers. Consult the manufacturer's instructions for a suggested rough-out opening to accommodate a given window.

Header Size: (4x or built-up 2x)	Maximum Span in feet:
4x4	4'
4x6	6'
4x8	8'
4x10	10'
4x12	12'

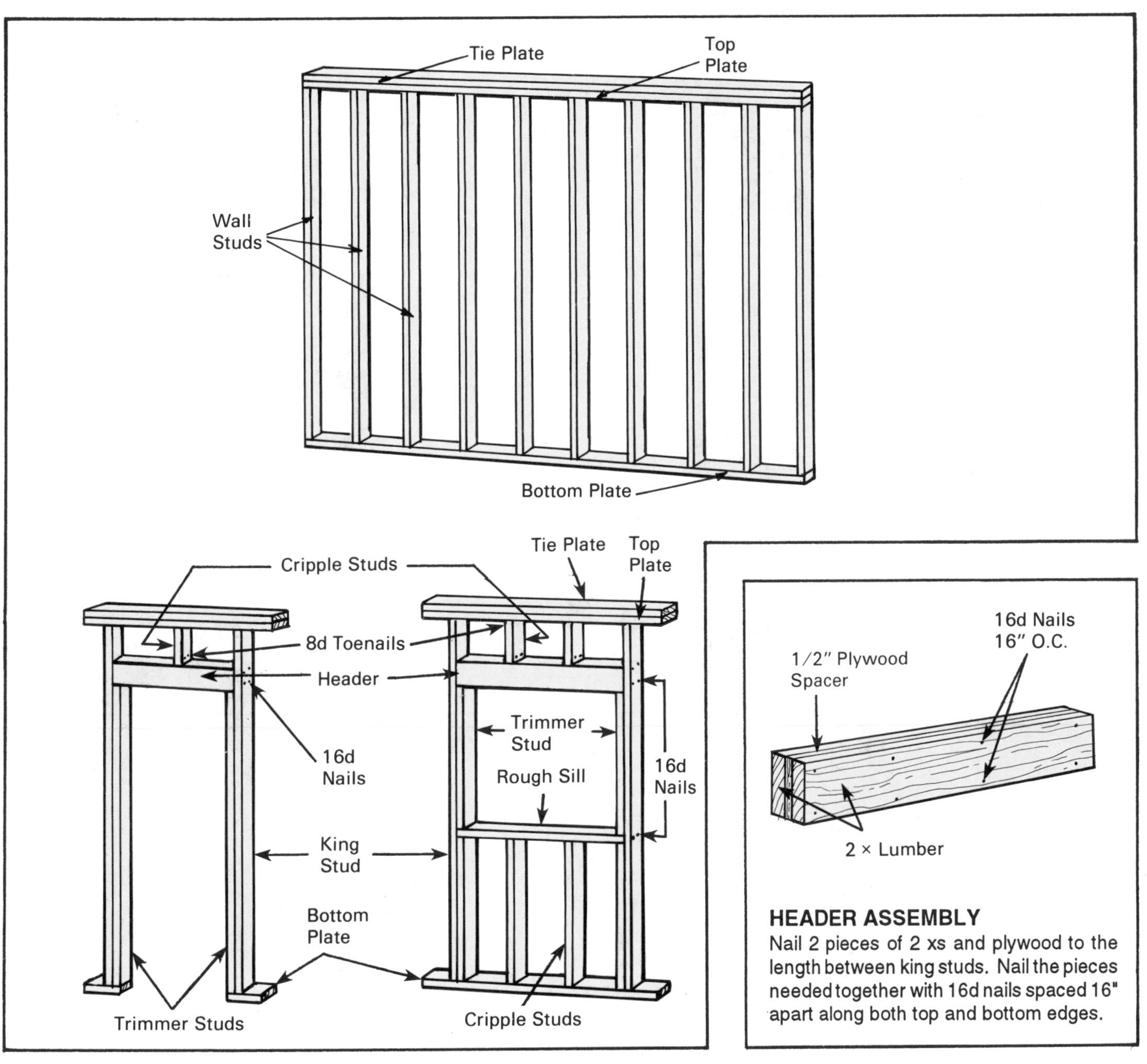

Figure 23-A Door and Window Framing

Diagonal Bracing

Structures with plywood siding normally do not require bracing, but all others do. The two most commonly used types of bracing are wooden "let-in" bracing made of 1x4 stock and metal strap bracing.

Let-in Bracing

This type of wooden bracing runs from the top outside corners of the wall to the bottom center of the wall. It forms a V-shaped configuration as shown on page 23. These braces are set into notched studs and are prepared while the wall frame is still lying on the slab.

Lay the 1x4 on the frame with one end at a top corner and the other end as far out on the bottom plate as possible without running into any door or window opening. Mark the underside of the brace where it overhangs the top and bottom plates to determine the angle at which the plates cross. Also mark both sides of the studs and plates at each point the brace crosses them. Notch the studs at these locations by making repeated cuts with your circular saw. Use a hammer and wood chisel to knock out any stubborn chips. Trim the ends of the 1x4 and put the brace in place. Hold it in place with a single nail until the wall is raised and plumbed. Then nail the brace fast with 8d nails wherever it crosses a plate or stud.

Metal Strap Bracing

Commonly available in 10' to 12' lengths, this type of bracing is nailed to the outside of the studded walls after they are raised, square, and plumb. Metal bracing is thin enough not to obstruct the exterior wall sheathing.

The straps have predrilled holes every 2" sized to accept an 8d nail. Strap bracing must always be installed in crossed pairs, similar to a large **X** design.

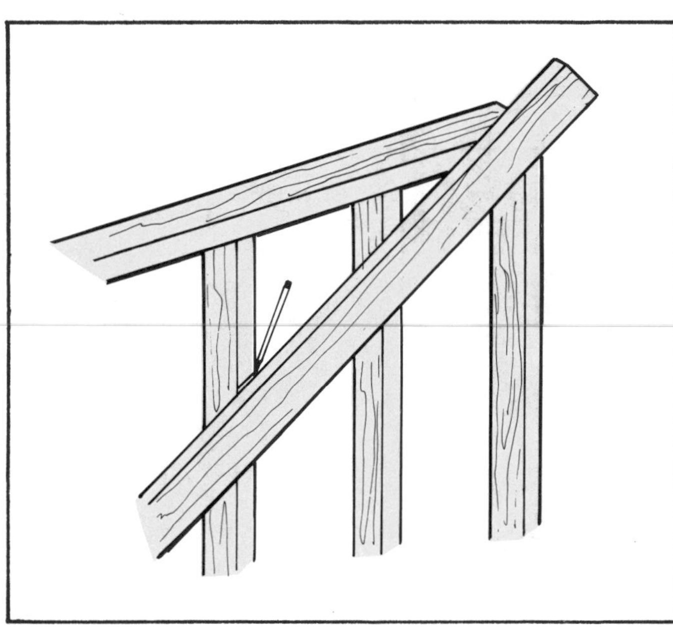

STEP 1 Mark bracing locations.

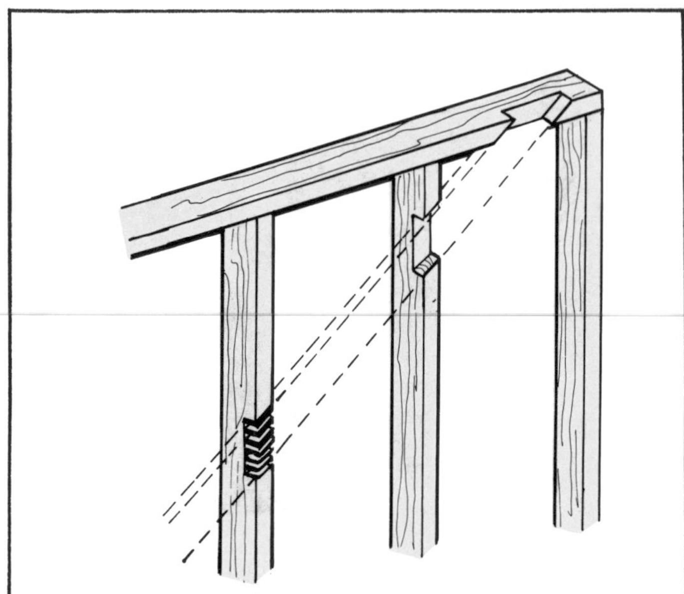

STEP 2 Notch out studs.

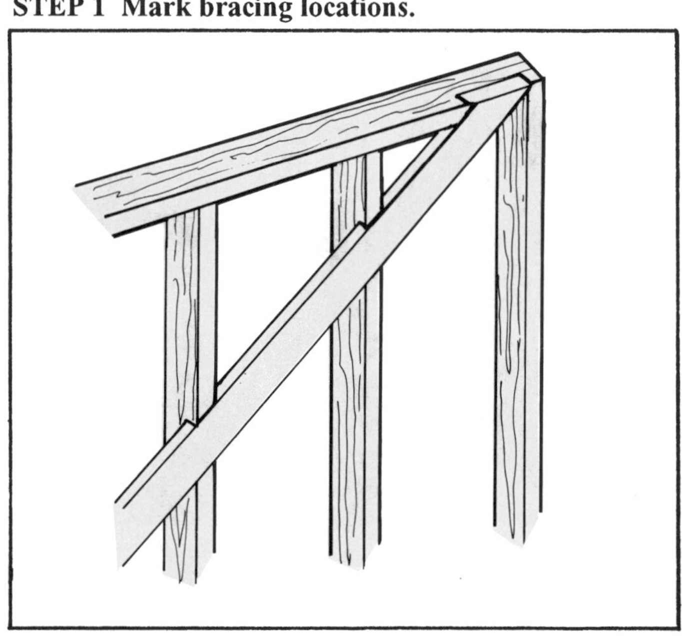

STEP 3 Nail bracing into stud locations.

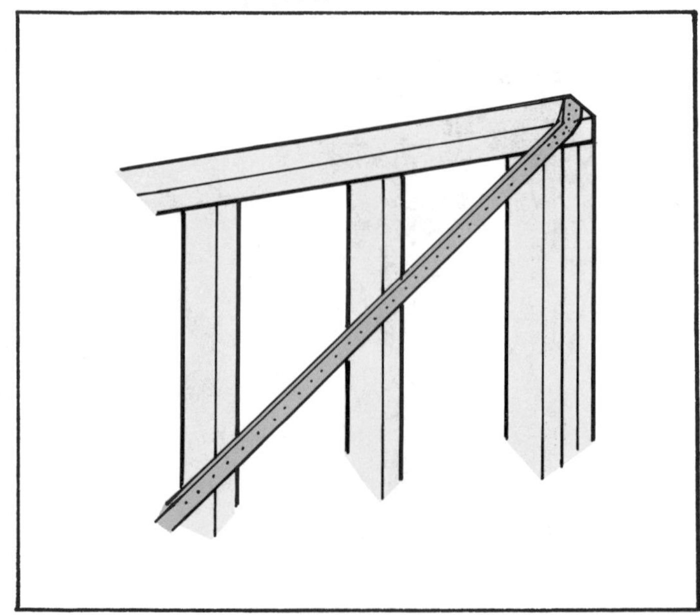

Alternate Metal Strap

Raising the Walls

Most walls can be raised by hand if enough help is available on the job site. It is advisable to have one person for every 10' of wall for the lifting operation.

The order in which walls are framed and raised can vary from job to job, but in general, the longer exterior walls are framed first. The shorter exterior walls are then raised and the corners are nailed together.

Once the first wall is framed out, there are only a few short steps until it is up and standing. If you are raising a wall on a slab, slide the wall along the slab until the bottom plate lies near the anchor bolt at the floor's edge. If you are raising a wall on a wood floor, you might want to tack some scrap lumber along the floor rim joists to prevent the wall from slipping over the edge. To raise the wall have your workers grip it at the top plate in unison and work their hands beneath the plate. Now everyone walks down the wall until it is in the upright position. On a slab you need to slip the bottom plate in place over the anchor bolts as you tilt the wall up.

To brace the wall, tack 2x4 braces to the wall studs, one at each end and one in the middle if the wall is particularly long. Tie these braces into stakes driven firmly into the ground or tack them to the wood floor rim joists if appropriate. Secure the wall by using washers and nuts if you have anchor bolts or tack the bottom plate to the wood floor. ***Do not securely nail the bottom plate to the floor until you are certain that the wall is in proper alignment.***

To check alignment, use a carpenter's level to check the wall for plumb along both end studs on adjacent faces. If the wall is out of plumb, loosen that brace, align the wall, and secure the brace again. If an end stud is warped, bridge the warp with a straight board. When both ends are plumb, adjust the middle.

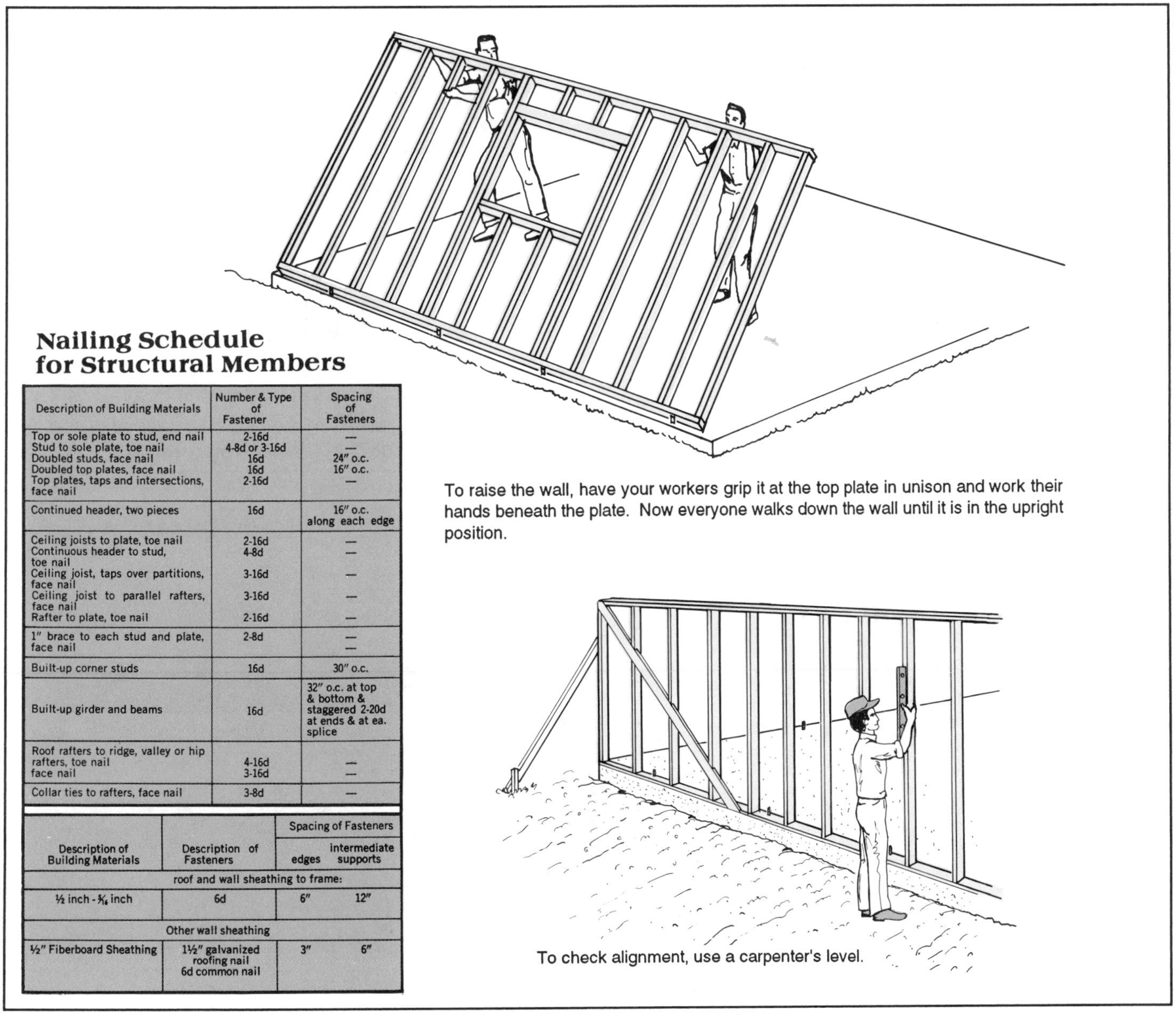

Nailing Schedule for Structural Members

Description of Building Materials	Number & Type of Fastener	Spacing of Fasteners
Top or sole plate to stud, end nail	2-16d	—
Stud to sole plate, toe nail	4-8d or 3-16d	—
Doubled studs, face nail	16d	24" o.c.
Doubled top plates, face nail	16d	16" o.c.
Top plates, taps and intersections, face nail	2-16d	—
Continued header, two pieces	16d	16" o.c. along each edge
Ceiling joists to plate, toe nail	2-16d	—
Continuous header to stud, toe nail	4-8d	—
Ceiling joist, taps over partitions, face nail	3-16d	—
Ceiling joist to parallel rafters, face nail	3-16d	—
Rafter to plate, toe nail	2-16d	—
1" brace to each stud and plate, face nail	2-8d	— —
Built-up corner studs	16d	30" o.c.
Built-up girder and beams	16d	32" o.c. at top & bottom & staggered 2-20d at ends & at ea. splice
Roof rafters to ridge, valley or hip rafters, toe nail	4-16d	—
face nail	3-16d	—
Collar ties to rafters, face nail	3-8d	—

Description of Building Materials	Description of Fasteners	Spacing of Fasteners	
		edges	intermediate supports
roof and wall sheathing to frame:			
½ inch - 5/16 inch	6d	6"	12"
Other wall sheathing			
½" Fiberboard Sheathing	1½" galvanized roofing nail 6d common nail	3"	6"

To raise the wall, have your workers grip it at the top plate in unison and work their hands beneath the plate. Now everyone walks down the wall until it is in the upright position.

To check alignment, use a carpenter's level.

Leveling and Corner Details

Once raised, the wall should also be checked for levelness. If needed, it can be shimmed level using tapered cedar shingles driven between the foundation and the bottom plate. Once the wall is plumb and level, tighten the anchor nuts to their final tightness or on wooden floors nail two 16d common nails between each stud. Do *not* nail the bottom plate in a door opening since this section must be cut out for the door.

At corners, nail through the end walls into the stud using 16d common nails staggered every 12". When the walls are up, you can then add the 2x4 tie plates to the top plates on each wall. These tie plates lap over onto adjacent walls to interlock the walls and give added strength to the structure.

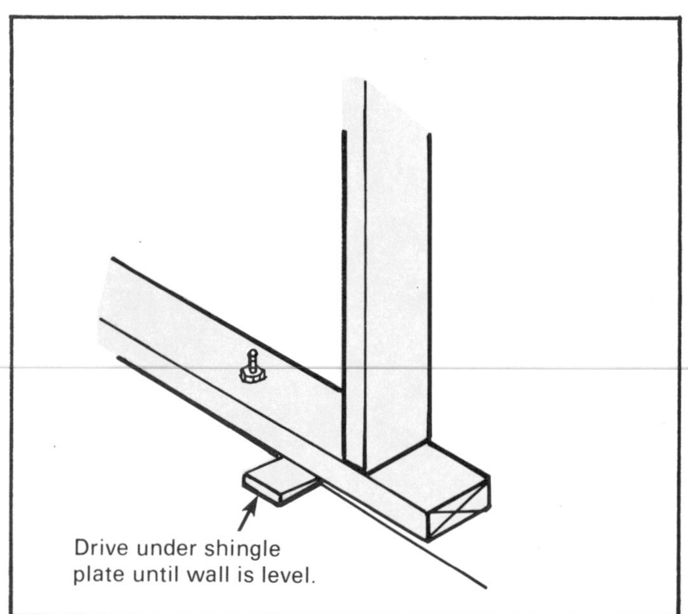

Figure 26-A Leveling the wall

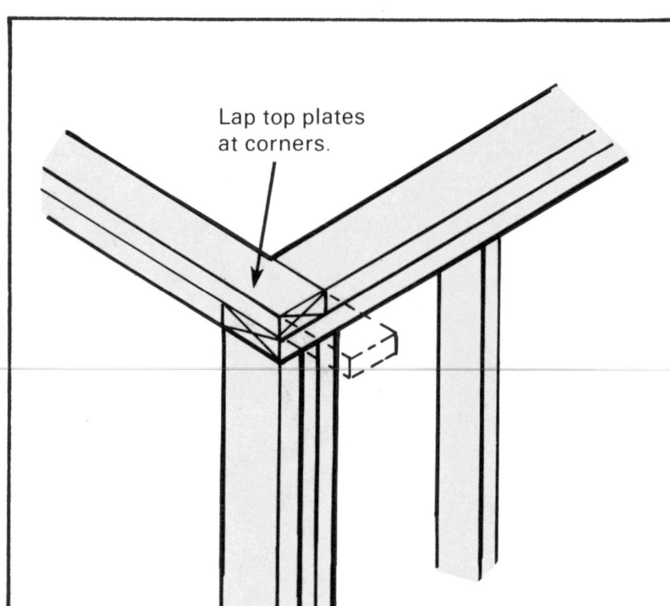

Figure 26-B Corner Detail Top Plates

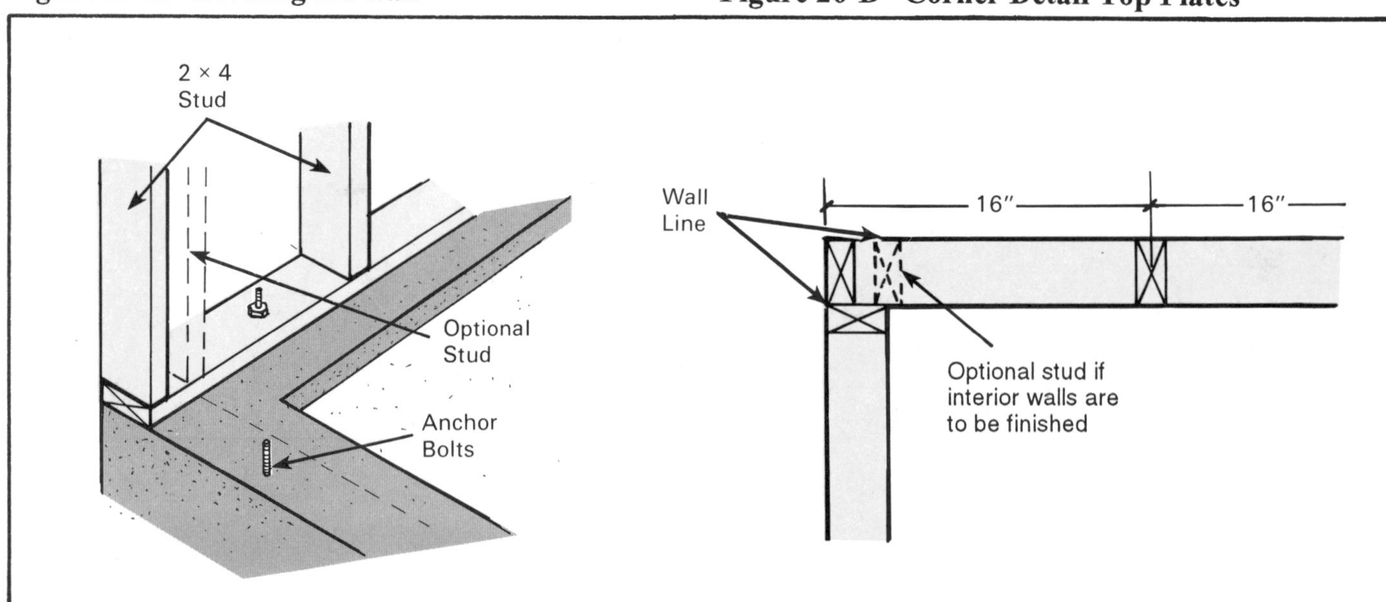

Figure 26-C Corner Details

Roof Framing

Most roof designs are variations of the **gable roof**, in which evenly spaced pairs of **common rafters** join the tie plates and central ridge board together. A **hip roof** is also used in shed construction and most often utilizes small hip roof trusses to create the roof framing. Rafters are 2x4's, 2x6's, or 2x8's depending upon span, spacing, load, and roof slope. They are installed on 16" or 24" centers. Check with your local building department for help regarding rafter requirements and roof load in your area. At the peak, rafter boards butt against a central ridge board. The **ridge board** can be either 1by or 2by lumber and is one size wider than the rafter lumber. Slope, or pitch, is referred to in terms of **unit rise** in a given **unit run**. Unit run is fixed at 12 inches. Unit rise is the slope over those 12 inches. A rise of 4" over 12" equals a slope of "4 in 12."

Cutting the Rafters

A common rafter has three cuts: the **plumb cut** to form the angle where the rafter meets the ridge board, the **bird's mouth notch** to fit the top plate, and the **tail cut** at the end of the overhang. Professionally prepared plans often have a template or diagram that serves as a master for rafter cutting. Cut two rafters off the master and check them for accuracy before using the others. Use a steel carpenter's square to mark the cuts.

Raising the Roof

With ridge board and rafters cut, you can raise the roof. Unless the roof is small, you'll need three people. Nail an upright 2x4 for each of the end rafters flush against the middle of the end top plate. One person then lines up one end rafter with the end of the side top plate and ties it in with three 16d nails. The second raises and holds it at the correct slope against one of the 2x4's, while the third tacks the two together. Do the same with the opposite end rafter, then align the ridge board between the top of the rafters and tie it in with three 16d common nails through each rafter. Use 8d common nails if the ridge board is 1by common lumber. The ridge board must be level, and the rafter ends must be flush with the sides of the ridge board. Repeat the process at the opposite end for a single-piece ridge board. For a two-piece ridge board, connect the rafters to the last spacing mark at the opposite end.

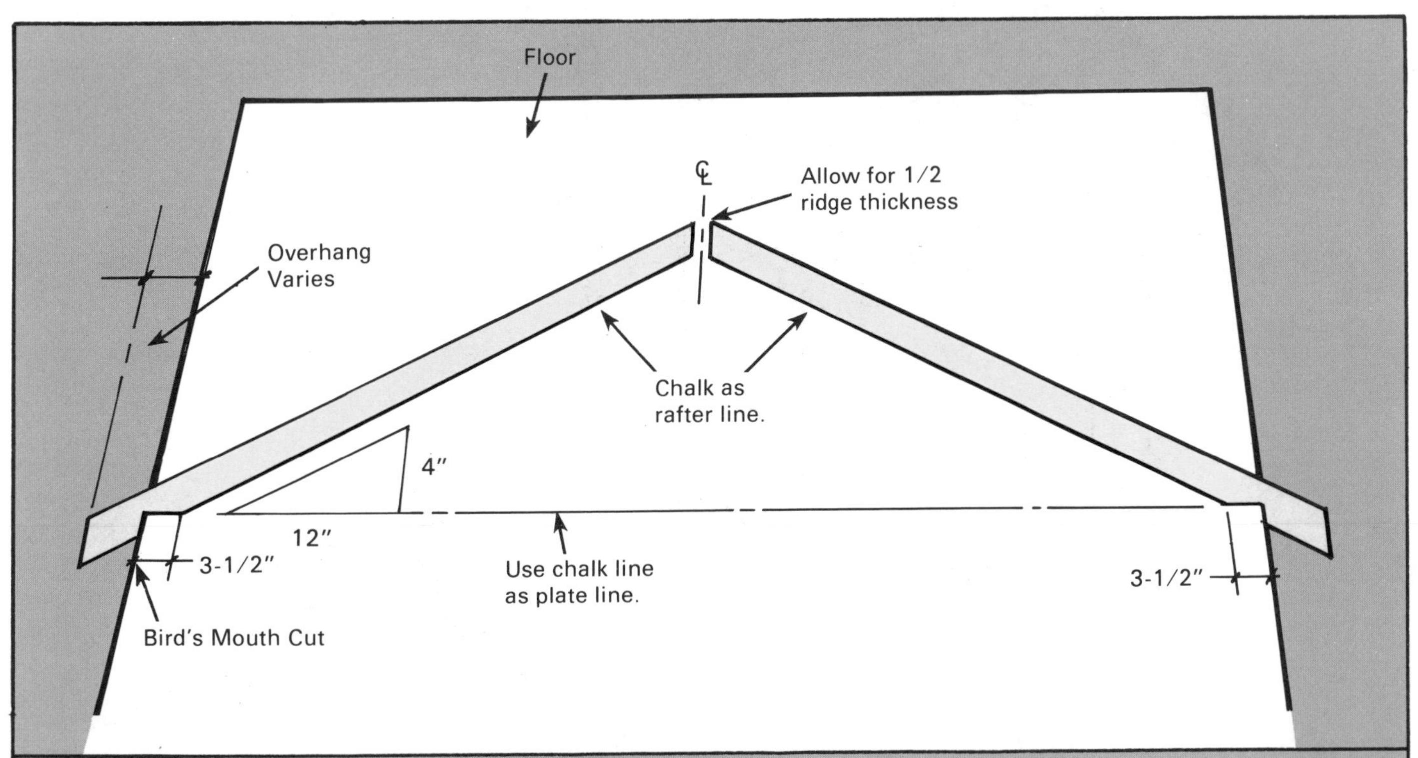

For those not familiar with a square, lay out the initial pair of rafters on the slab or wooden floor. Snap chalk lines to represent the bottom of the rafters and the plate line. Use the rise in 12" to establish the angle (for example, 4" in 12"). If they fit, use them as patterns for all other rafters.

Erecting the Rafters

Make sure the end rafters are plumb and that the ridge board is level and centered mid-span. Next attach a diagonal brace between the ridge board and the 2x4 nailed to the top plate. Run the remaining rafters in pairs, attaching them to the ridge board first, then to the top plate (See figures 28 A & B). If your local codes require seismic/hurricane anchors, use metal connectors to secure the rafters to the top plate.

If a second ridge board is used, the process is repeated from the opposite end of the building. The junction of the ridge boards must be covered by two rafters. If you plan to install rafter ties (or ceiling joists), use three 16d nails to tie rafters to the rafter ties and cut the ties to match the slope of the rafters.

Be sure to add collar ties and hangers before removing any shoring or bracing.

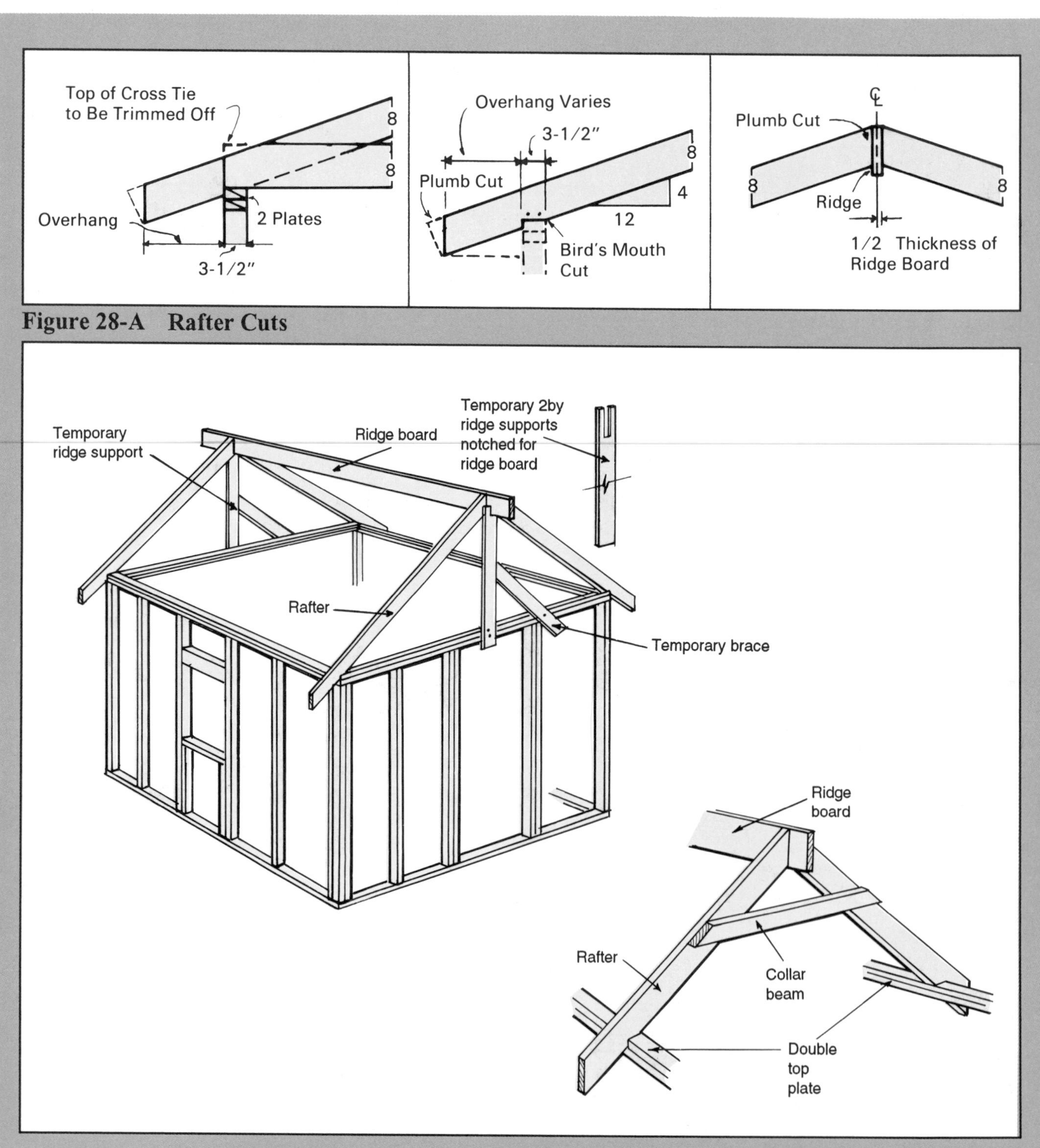

Figure 28-A Rafter Cuts

Figure 28-B Ridge Board Supports

Using Metal Connectors for Roof Framing

As mentioned earlier, metal fasteners provide the strength nails alone cannot provide. They also avoid the irritation of watching angled nails split the lumber which you have so carefully cut and fitted. Certain metal connectors allow the rafter to rest directly on the tie or top plate and eliminate the difficult and time-consuming bird's mouth cut.

Other connectors are designed to join the rafter to the ridge board without toenailing. As you can see from the illustrations below, many different types of metal connectors are available for roof framing work. While metal roof framing connectors will add some additional expense to your project, they will save you time and create a more durable shed.

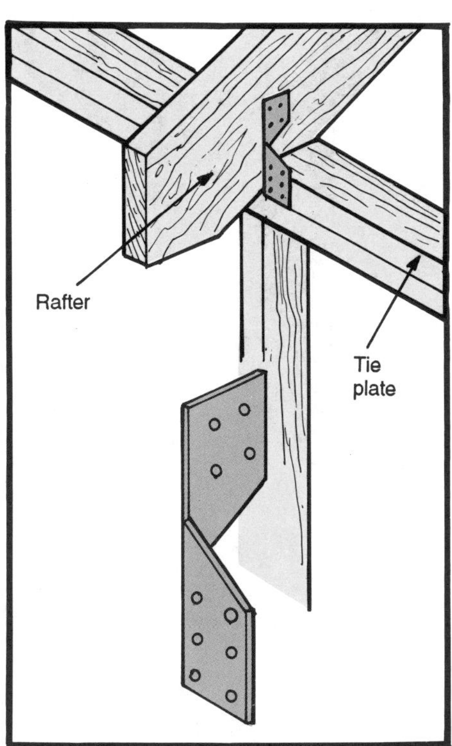

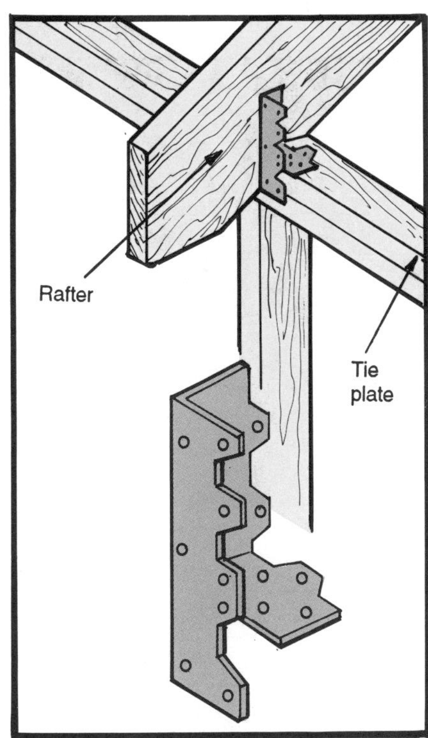

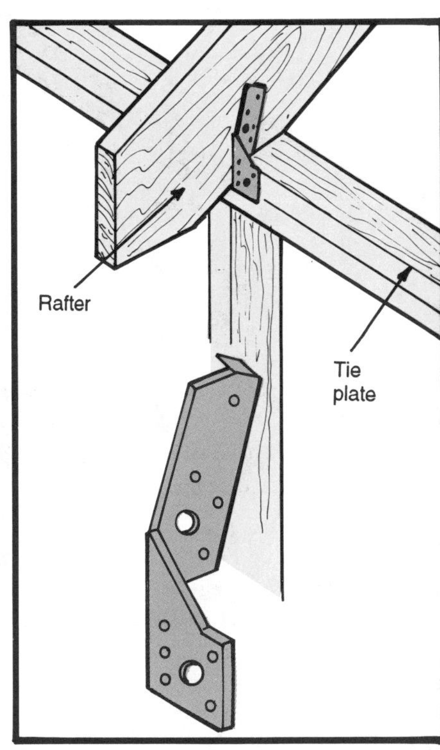

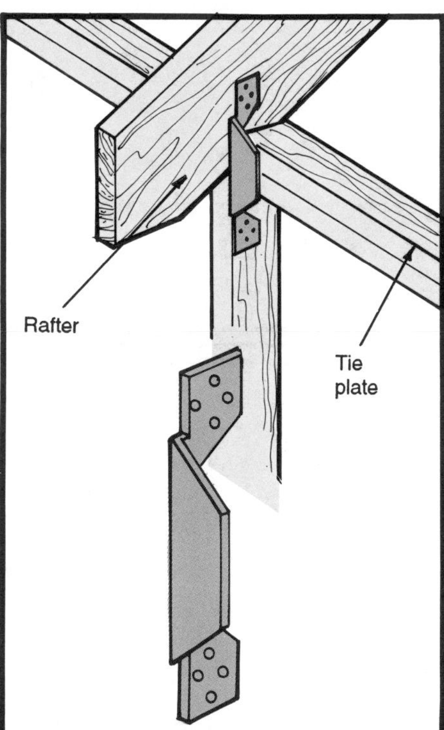

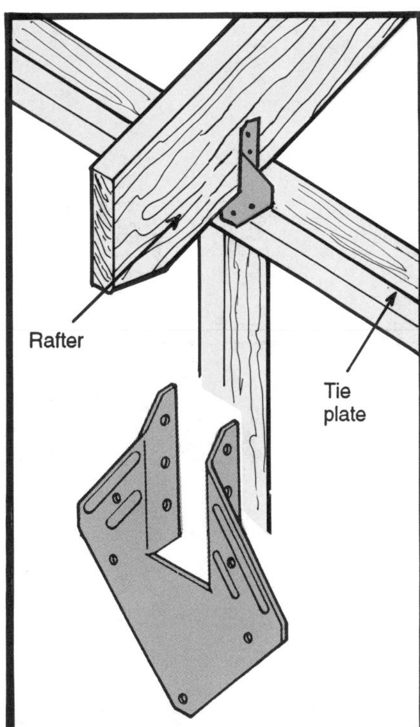

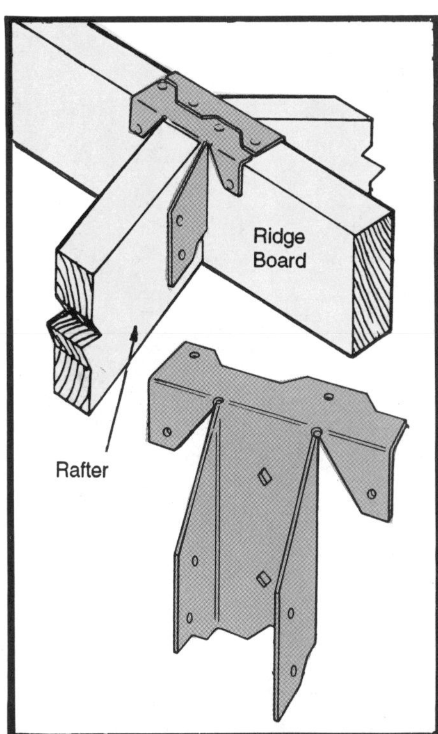

Some Illustrations courtesy of Simpson Strong-Tie Co., Inc.

Roof Framing (Continued)

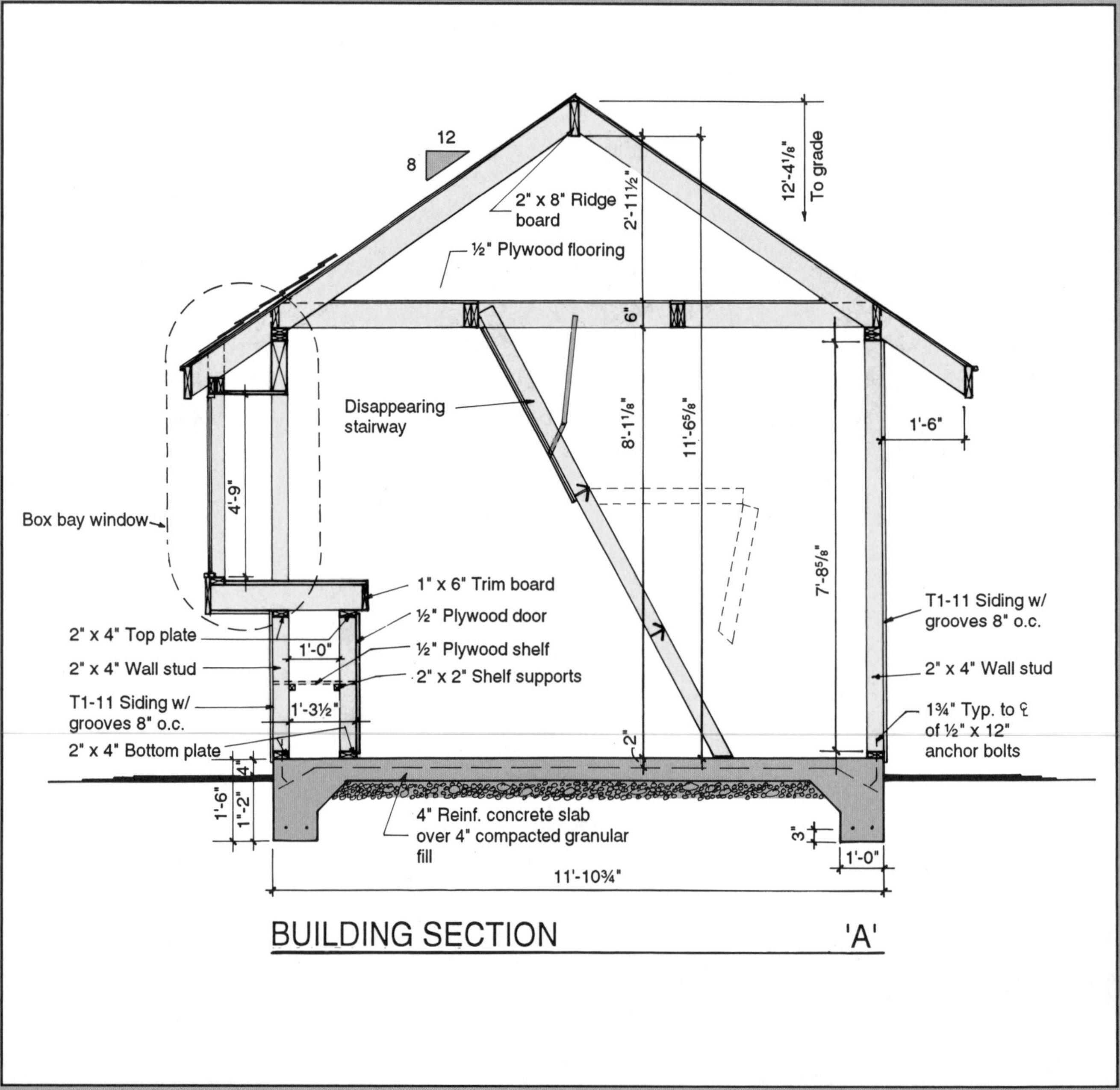

12
8
2" x 8" Ridge board
½" Plywood flooring
2'-11½"
12'-4⅛"
To grade
6"
Disappearing stairway
8'-1⅛"
11'-6⅝"
1'-6"
Box bay window
4'-9"
7'-8⅝"
1" x 6" Trim board
½" Plywood door
½" Plywood shelf
2" x 2" Shelf supports
2" x 4" Top plate
2" x 4" Wall stud
T1-11 Siding w/ grooves 8" o.c.
2" x 4" Bottom plate
1'-0"
1'-3½"
T1-11 Siding w/ grooves 8" o.c.
2" x 4" Wall stud
1¾" Typ. to ℄ of ½" x 12" anchor bolts
2"
4"
1'-6"
1'-2"
4" Reinf. concrete slab over 4" compacted granular fill
3"
1'-0"
11'-10¾"
BUILDING SECTION 'A'

Typical Shed Wall Section

8'-10"
3²¹/₃₂"
8'-7⁵/₃₂"
5½"
Secondary cut for rafters over box bay window, only
1³/₁₆"
1³/₁₆"
2³/₈"
3½"
See detail below for additional dimensions
2" x 6" Rafter
3⁵/₈"
2³/₁₆"
1'-9⁵/₁₆"
4³/₁₆"
6'-8²¹/₃₂"
3²¹/₃₂"
1¼"
2⁵/₁₆"
2"

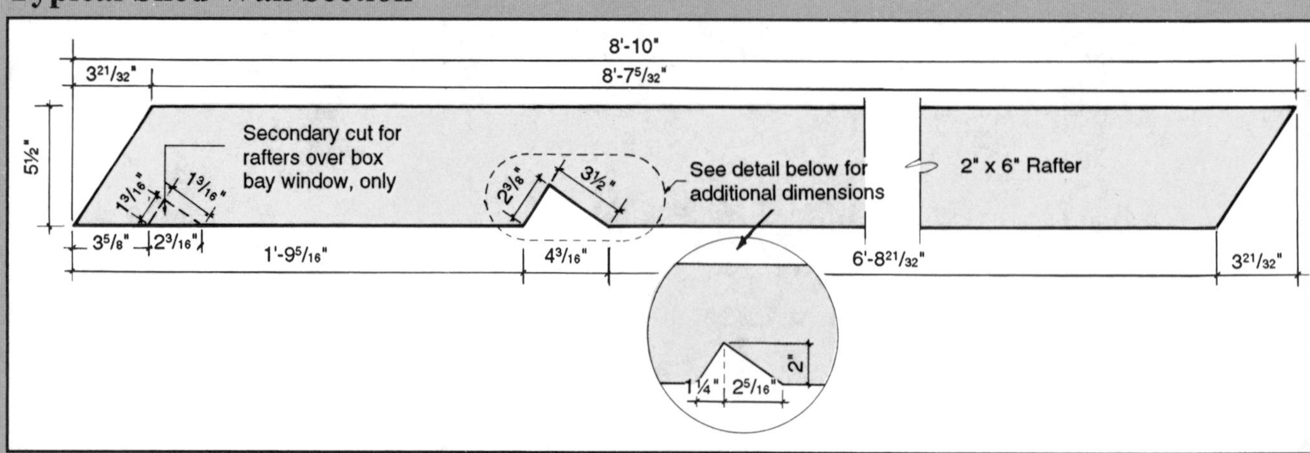

Typical Rafter Cutting Diagram

Variations of the Roof Cornice

Whatever type of roof you decide to construct, your building will have a roof overhang to protect the top of the side walls from moisture penetration. This overhang is generally known as the roof cornice. The cornice can also serve to provide ventilation and protection from the hot overhead rays of the sun on the sidewalls. As a general rule of thumb, warmer climates tend to favor longer overhangs which offer greater shading.

An open cornice is illustrated in Figure 31-A. The overhang can extend up to 24" from the edge of the building. You have the option of adding a frieze board to the rafter ends or leaving the rafter ends exposed. Remember that when you create an exposed overhang, the roof sheathing is visible from underneath. Painting or staining the sheathing can improve its appearance.

Figure 31-B represents a closed cornice. Make a seat cut on the rafter at the top plate. Cut the rafter ends flush and vertical with the top plate. Bring the siding all the way up to the rafters and finish off the cornice with a trim piece that covers the slightly exposed roof sheathing.

Two variations of the boxed cornice are shown in Figures 31-C and 31-D. A fascia board at the rafter ends is essential for any style of boxed cornice. Figure 31-C demonstrates the sloping soffit design where the rafters are used to directly attach the soffit board. Nail a 1by fascia to the square cut rafter ends. Another frieze board covers the end portion of the soffit where it meets the wall siding.

Figure 31-D portrays the level soffit design which requires 2x4 horizontal lookouts facenailed at the rafter ends and toenailed to wall siding. Level soffits generally extend no more than 12"-15" from the building wall. The lookouts help to frame the soffit construction.

Proper ventilation is essential for the boxed cornice. Install soffit vents (typically 4"x8") at regular intervals along the soffit between the lookouts. Be sure to install the screened vents or you will have unintentionally created a birdhouse wherever you have an unscreened vent!

Ventilation

If you plan to use your shed as a work area where you will spend longer periods of time, consider installing either gable end vents or roof vents. Vents help to reduce interior temperatures during the summer and to minimize condensation during the winter months. Gable end vents should be installed at both gable ends of your roof to promote cross-ventilation.

The number of roof vents you will install depends upon the cubic footage of your building. Simply create a box frame between roof rafters and install the vent according to the manufacturer's instructions. Don't forget to flash and then caulk the vent after you have installed the roof sheathing and shingles.

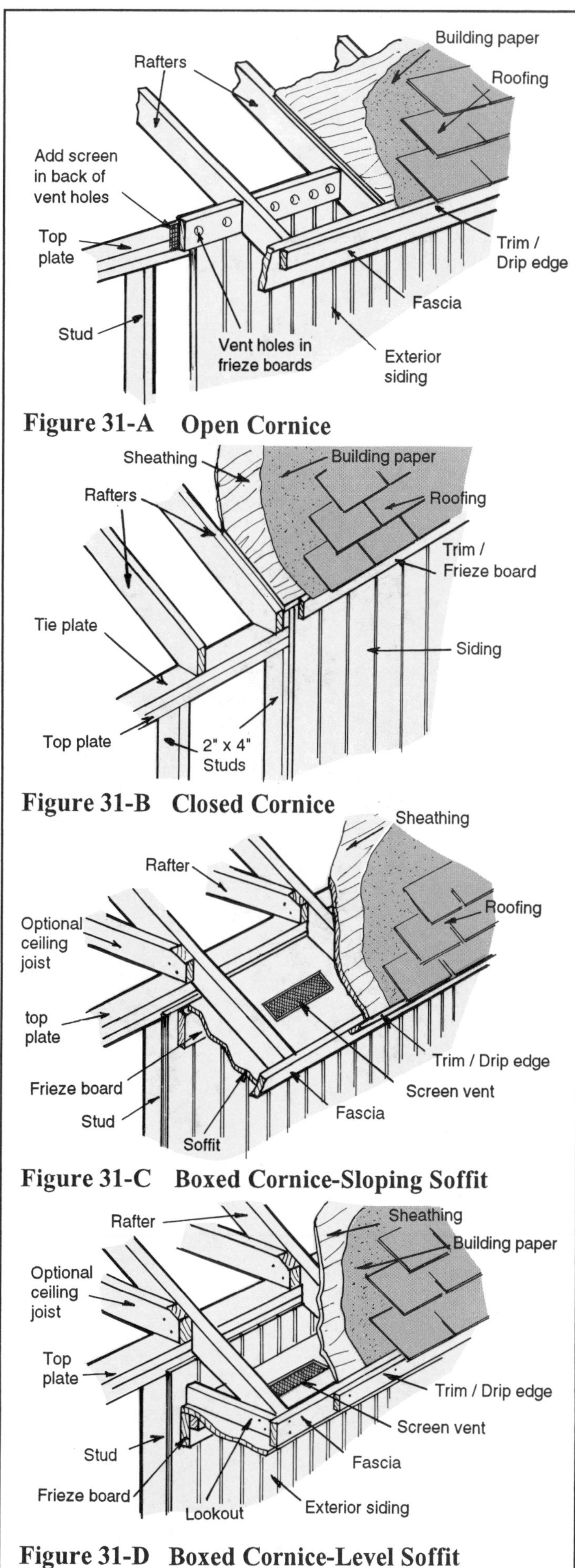

Figure 31-A Open Cornice

Figure 31-B Closed Cornice

Figure 31-C Boxed Cornice-Sloping Soffit

Figure 31-D Boxed Cornice-Level Soffit

Roof Sheathing

Use 4' x 8' plywood roof sheathing panels to create a strong base for your roofing material. The required thickness of sheathing will vary with rafter spacing and local building code requirements. Generally, the wider the rafter spacing, the thicker the sheathing needs to be. If you want the interior of your shed to have a finished look, use 2x6 tongue and groove material to create a solid roof sheathing and paint the underside.

Stagger the sheathing, starting at the bottom, so that the end joints of adjacent sheets fall on different rafters. Space 6d nails 6" apart at sheet ends and 12" on center at intermediate rafters. Leave a 1/16" expansion gap between the ends of sheets. For larger jobs, you might want to rent a pneumatic staple gun to fasten sheathing. If gable eaves have an overhang, be certain to extend the sheathing to cover it.

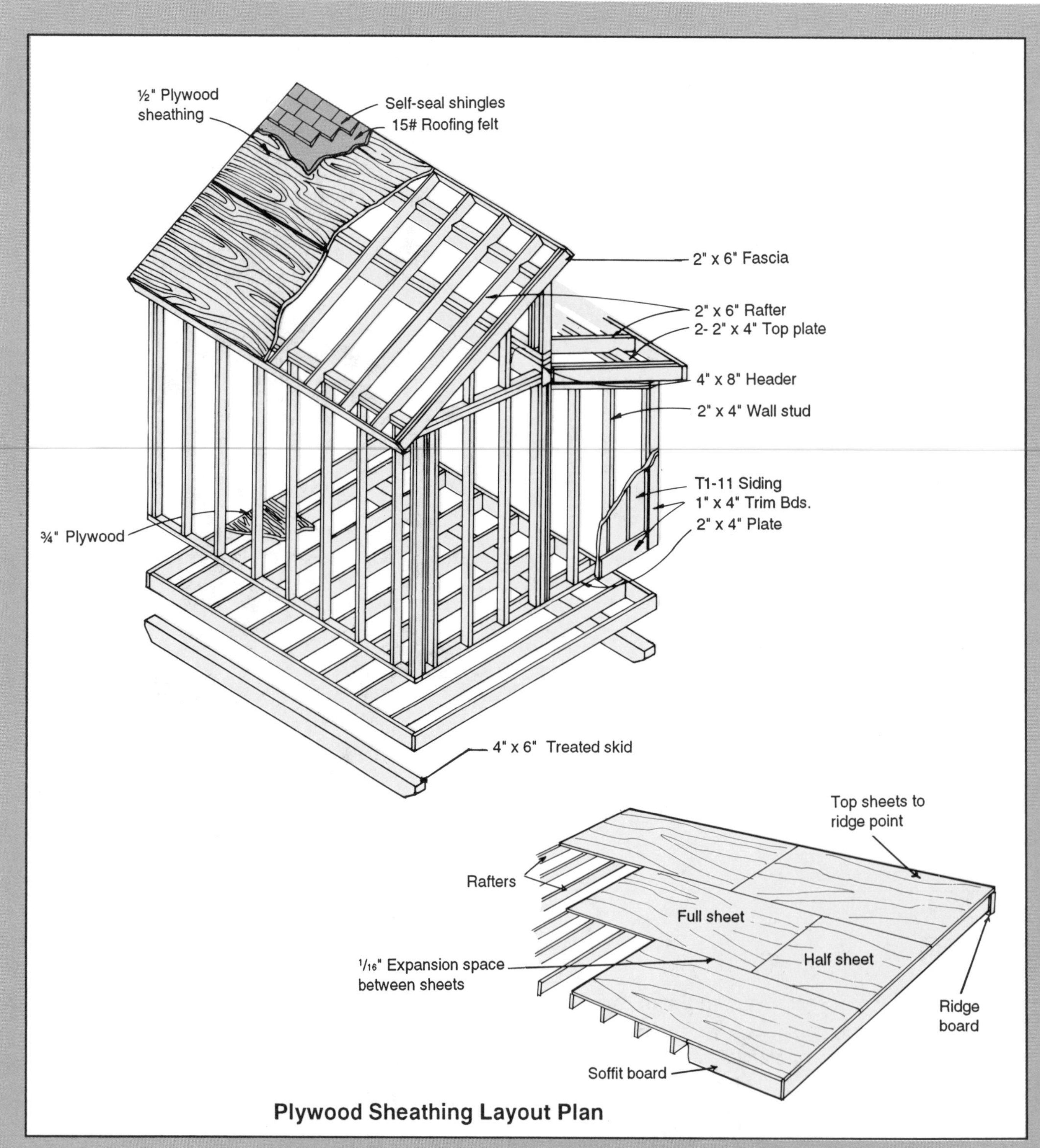

Plywood Sheathing Layout Plan

Gambrel Roof Construction

The gambrel roof offers an attractive barn-like alternative for shed design. Construct gambrel roof framing from trusses built on the ground and then erect the relatively lightweight trusses over wall framing.

To add additional strength to your gambrel roof trusses in areas with heavy snow loads, use truss plate connectors and truss tie-down brackets to connect the truss to the top plate.

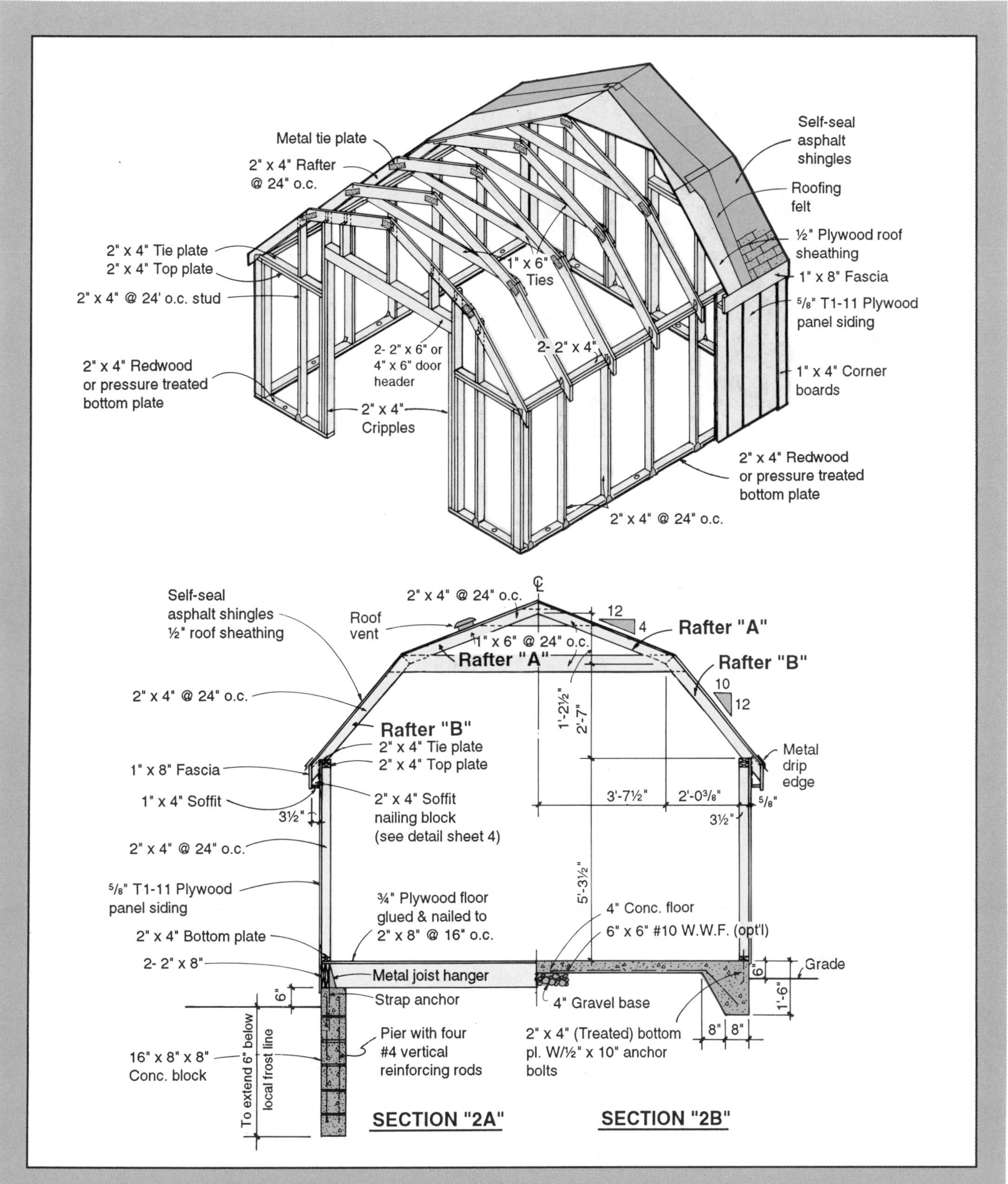

Shed Roof Construction

The shed roof lowers the height of one wall to create a lean-to appearance. Shed roofing is typical for buildings with clerestory windows like the design illustrated below. The advantage of the shed roof and clerestory window combination is that without wall windows all of your wall space is available for storage but you still have plenty of natural lighting provided by the windows above your workspace.

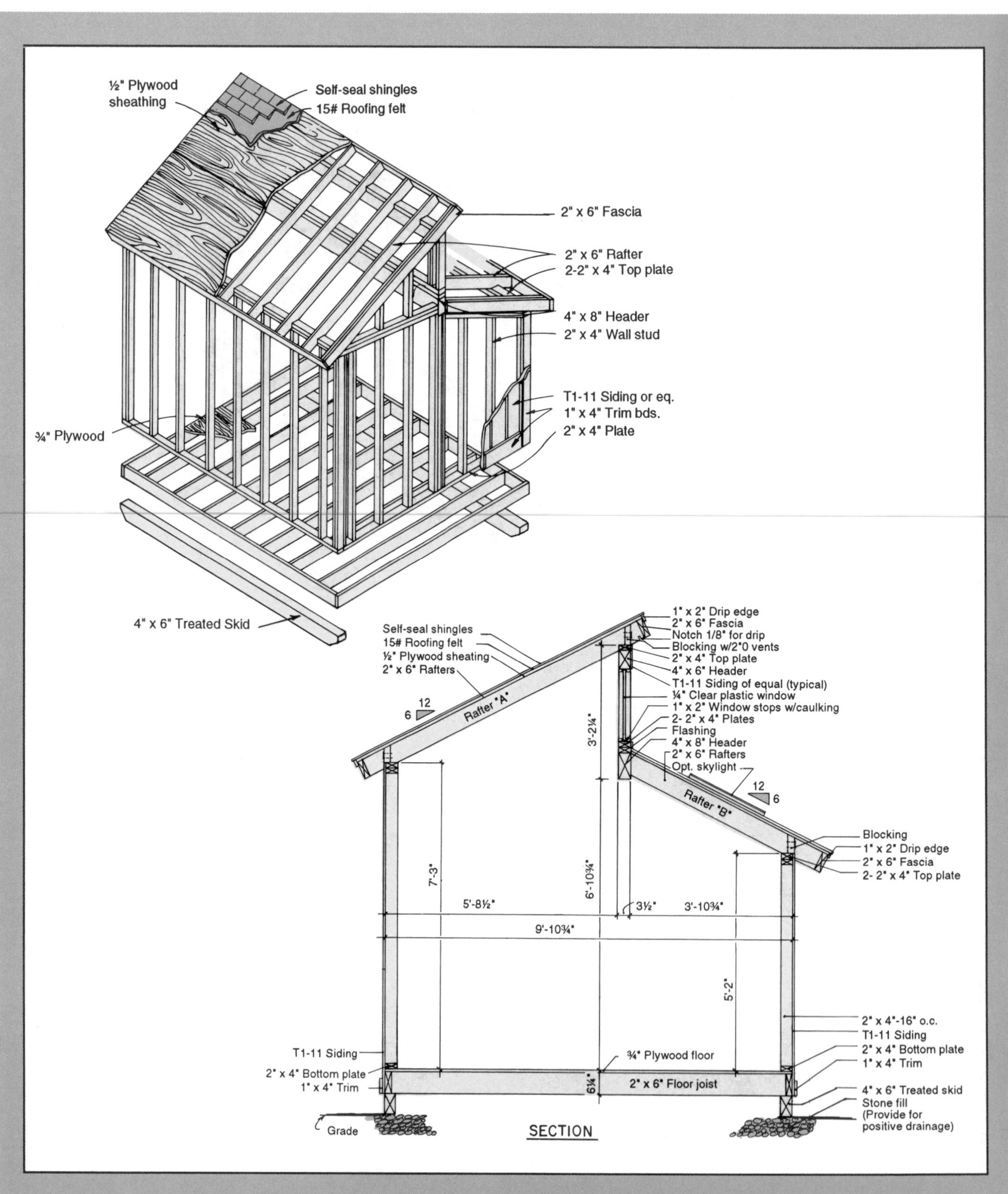

Applying Vertical Panel Siding

Before starting construction, select the siding and determine the need for wall sheathing. Wall sheathing requirements are determined by the stud spacing, the width of the door and window jambs, and the application of the trim (See figure 35-A).

A commonplace and inexpensive siding for sheds, T1-11 exterior siding does not require wall sheathing and adds structural strength. Flakeboard (Oriented Strand Board) is another inexpensive siding option for those with a tight budget. When you install vertical panel siding, nail 6d galvanized nails every 4"-6" at the edges of the panel and every 8"-12" inside the panel. You might be able to obtain siding nails that match the siding and thus eliminate painting both the siding and nails. If you have to add a panel above the bottom panel, use Z-bar flashing between the panels (See figure 35-C). Leave a ¼" gap around door and window openings when cutting siding to facilitate fitting.

When plywood sheathing is used, diagonal corner bracing can often be omitted. Decide whether trim is to be applied on top of the siding or butted into it. If butted, apply trim first, then apply siding. Horizontal wood siding is more expensive than plywood panel siding but provides an attractive and durable exterior. However, horizontal wood siding requires periodic painting for preservation.

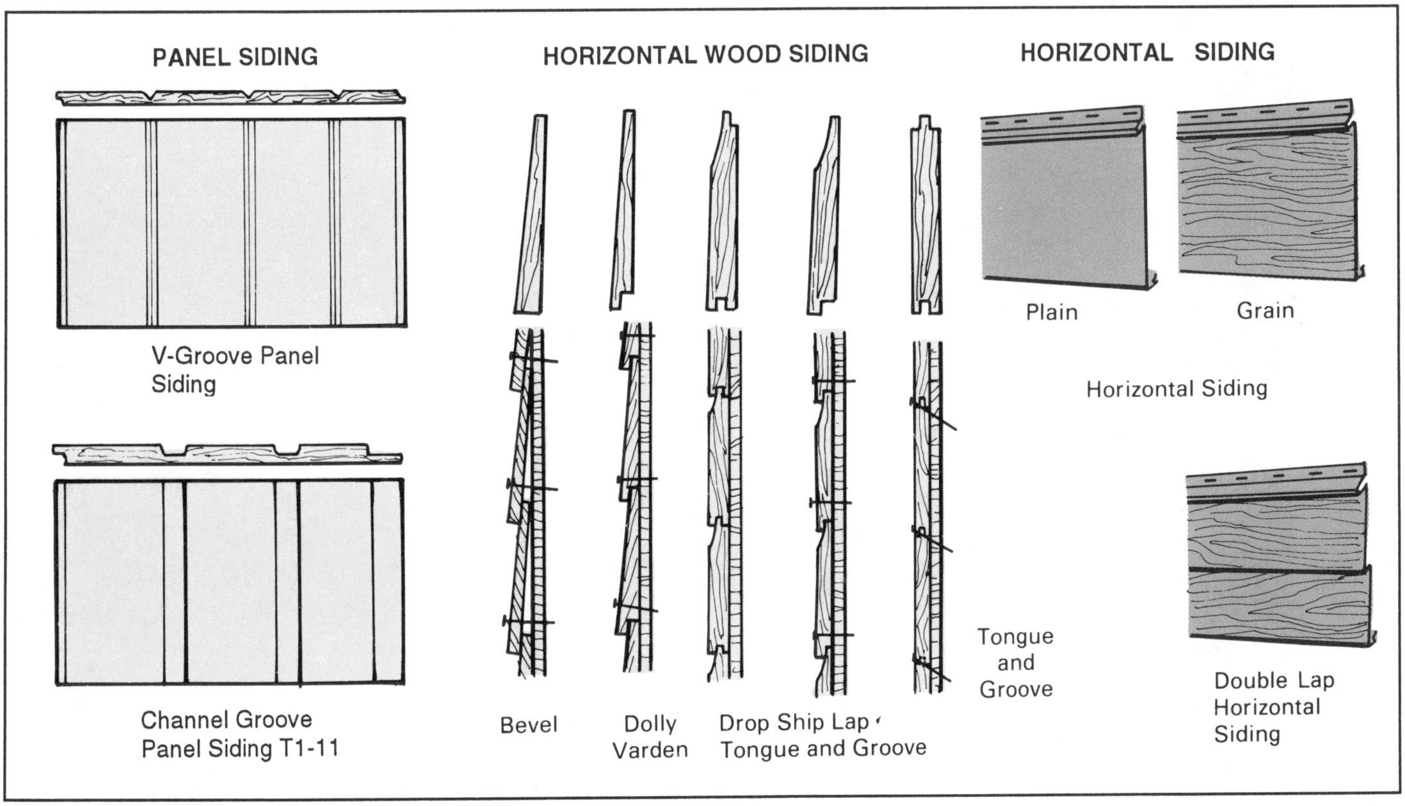

PANEL SIDING
V-Groove Panel Siding
Channel Groove Panel Siding T1-11

HORIZONTAL WOOD SIDING
Bevel
Dolly Varden
Drop Ship Lap Tongue and Groove
Tongue and Groove

HORIZONTAL SIDING
Plain
Grain
Horizontal Siding
Double Lap Horizontal Siding

Figure 35-A Siding Alternatives

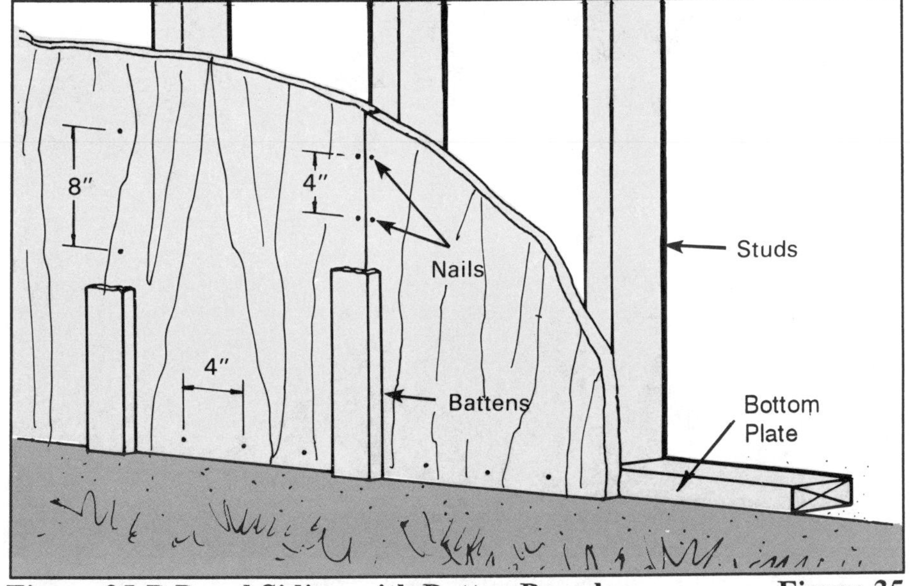

Figure 35-B Panel Siding with Batten Boards

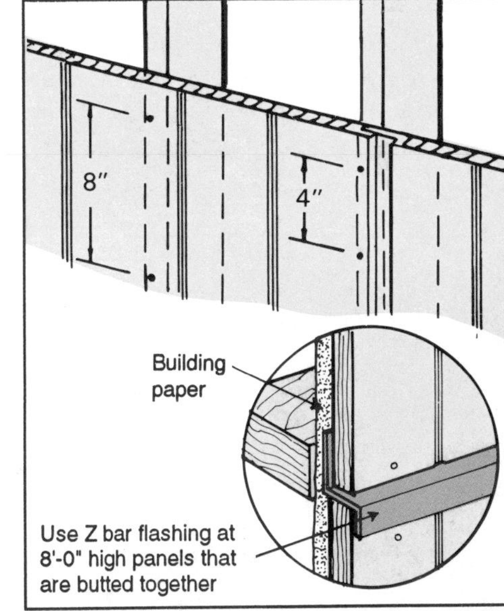

Figure 35-C Vertical Grooved Siding Panels

Applying Horizontal Hardboard Siding

Lay down various lengths of siding at each side. Apply so that joints in the succeeding course do not fall directly above each other. Butt all joints over the center of a stud. Seal by painting the edges with primer before butting. Start the bottom of the first course ½" below the bottom plate. Siding on all walls should be aligned and level and each course equally spaced. Be especially careful to determine the lap and exposure to the weather before applying the second and succeeding courses. Measure the distance to be covered and divide it by the desired exposure to get the total number of courses of siding. See Figure 36-B below. Carefully mark these spaces on the corners of each wall, taking into consideration the overlap of the siding. Run a chalk line from one mark to another, leaving a horizontal chalk line on the building paper as a guide. If you are not applying sheathing or building paper, chalk the wall studs directly. Apply the siding and keep it consistent by checking with your level.

Final openings, where siding meets the soffit if applicable, can be closed with a piece of quarter round or shingle mould. Protect your shed by painting or staining it as soon as possible.

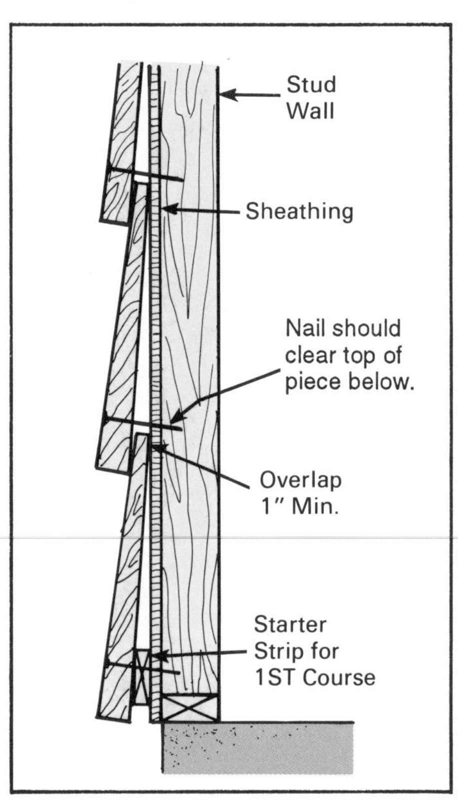

Figure 36-A Horizontal Siding Detail

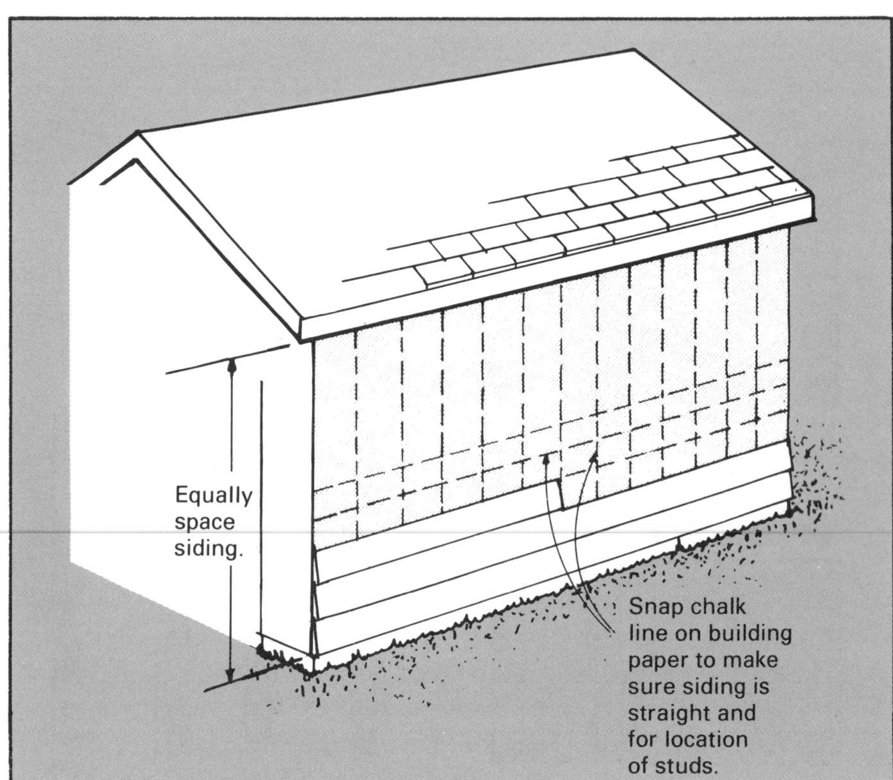

Figure 36-B Marking Siding Courses

Building Paper

Some local building codes might require that building paper be used to seal the wall from the elements. Building paper is typically felt or kraft paper impregnated with asphalt and is stapled or nailed between the siding and the sheathing or studs. Rolls are usually 36" wide and come in lengths covering between 200 to 500 square feet. Apply building paper in horizontal strips from the bottom of the wall as shown in Figure 36C. Overlaps should be 2" at horizontal joints, 6" at vertical joints, and 12" at corners. Cutting is done with a utility knife. Use just enough staples or nails in an installation to hold the paper in place. Siding nails will hold it permanently. Before your install siding, snap a level chalk line on the siding to indicate the bottom edge of the paper and work up.

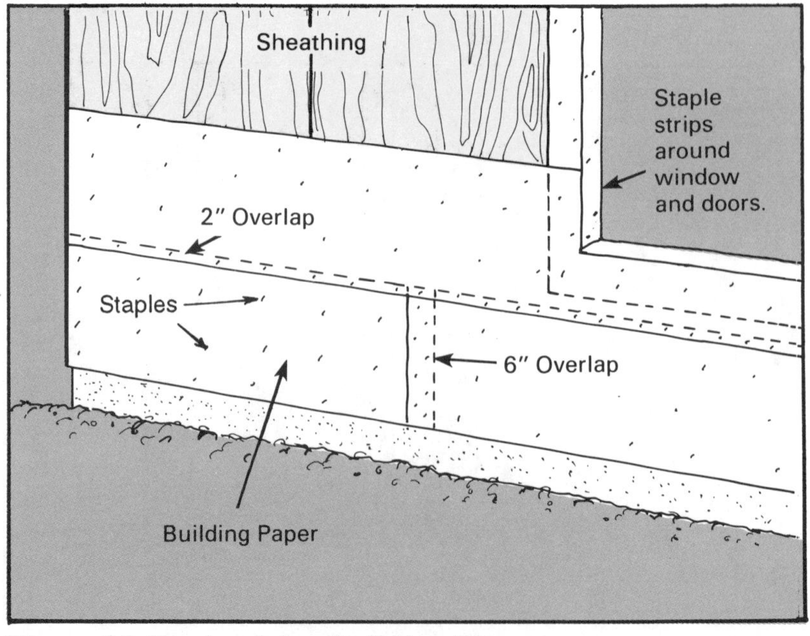

Figure 36-C Applying Building Paper

Overhang Details

Before applying trim, know the nailing requirements of the siding you select. Some siding will have trim applied over the siding, but other siding will butt against trim and require extra blocking at the edges. After the roof sheathing is on but before you install the fascia and rake boards, add soffit nailers if required. Use the longest fascia boards on the longest walls. Join all ends over the center of a rafter or nailer. Consult Figures 37-A to 37-F below. At the gable end, extend the fascia (or rake board) along the edge of the roof sheathing and rafter. At the top, cut the end to the angle of the rafter and butt at the center. Be sure to prime coat both ends before butting. At the lower end, let the front rake fascia extend beyond the side fascia, then cut the ends to line up with the side fascia.

Optional
Gutter
Rafter
Fascia
Nailer
Soffit

Figure 37-A Boxed Cornice Detail

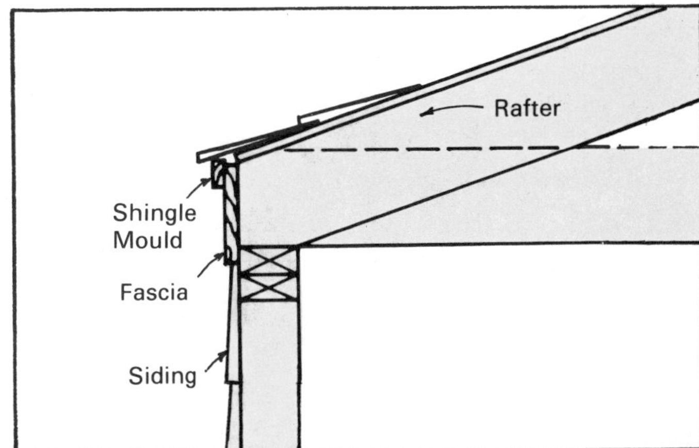

Figure 37-B Closed Cornice Detail

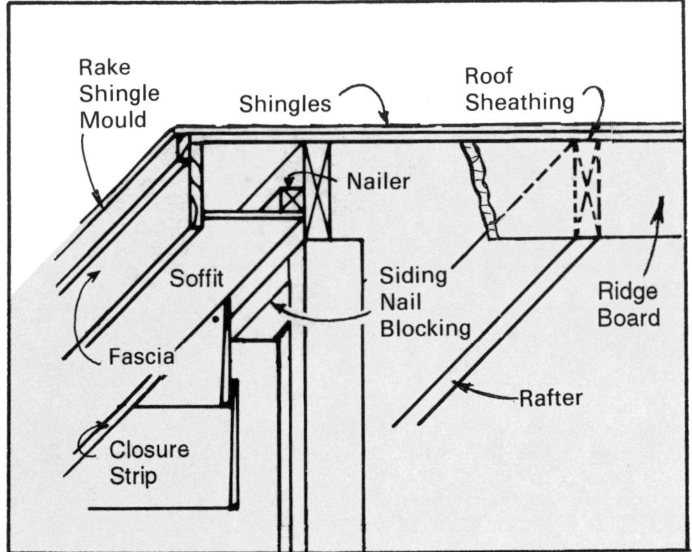

Figure 37-C Gable End Ridge Detail Box Overhang

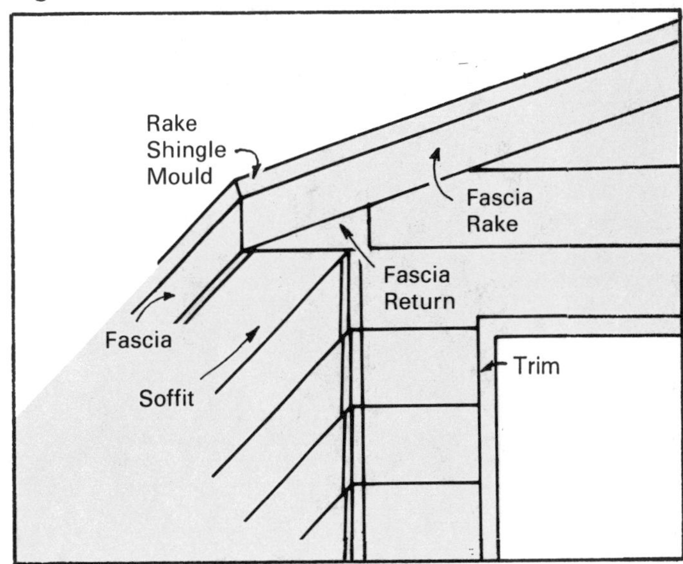

Figure 37-D Eave Detail Box Overhang

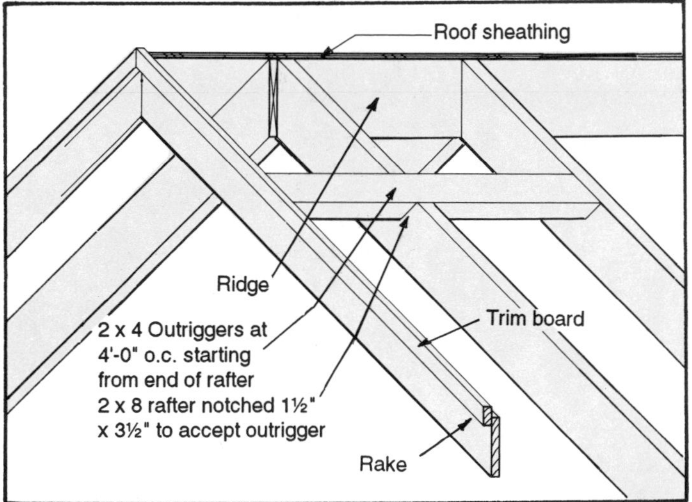

Figure 37-E Gable End Ridge Detail Open Overhang

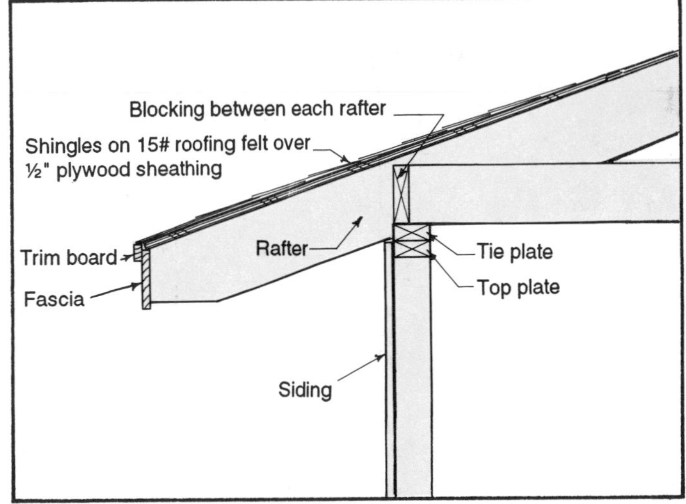

Figure 37-F Open Cornice Overhang

Corner Trim Details

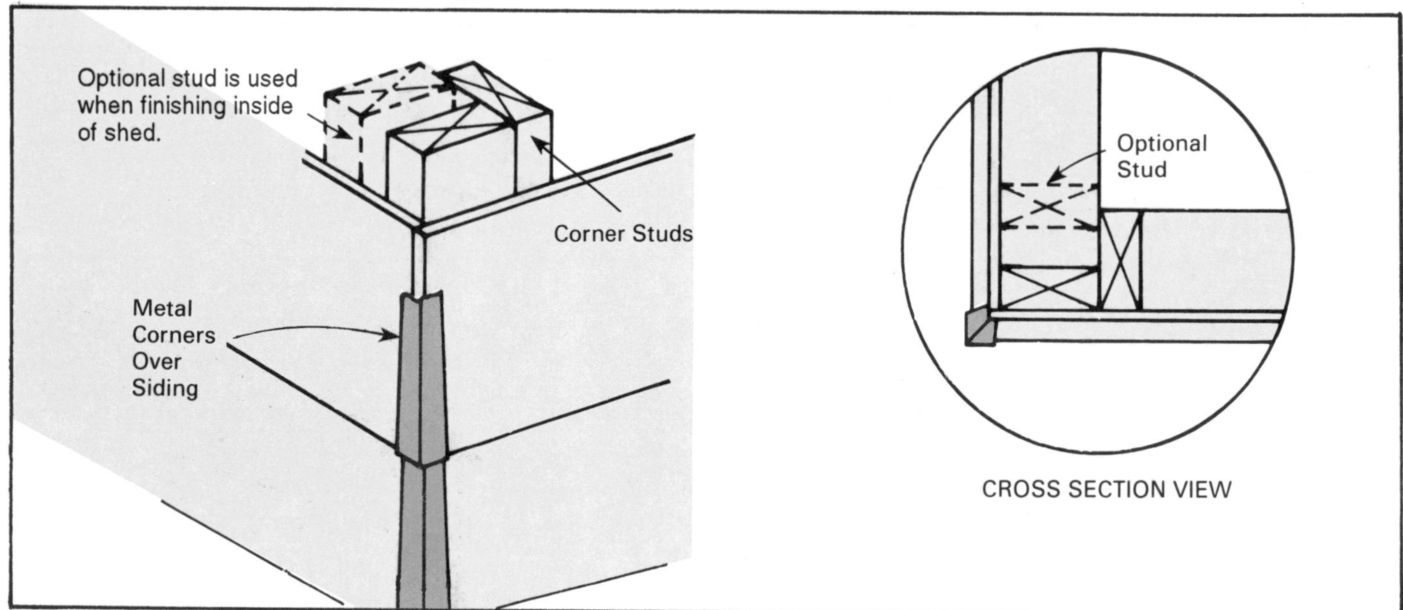

Figure 38-A Corner Tins

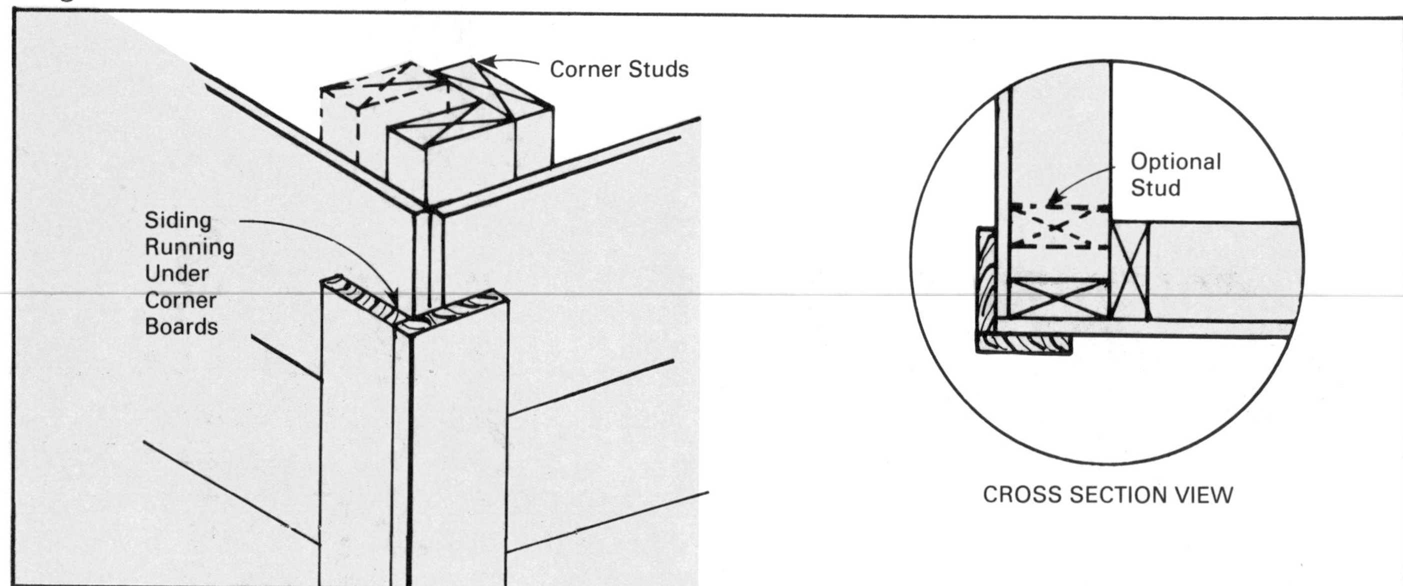

Figure 38-B Corner Boards

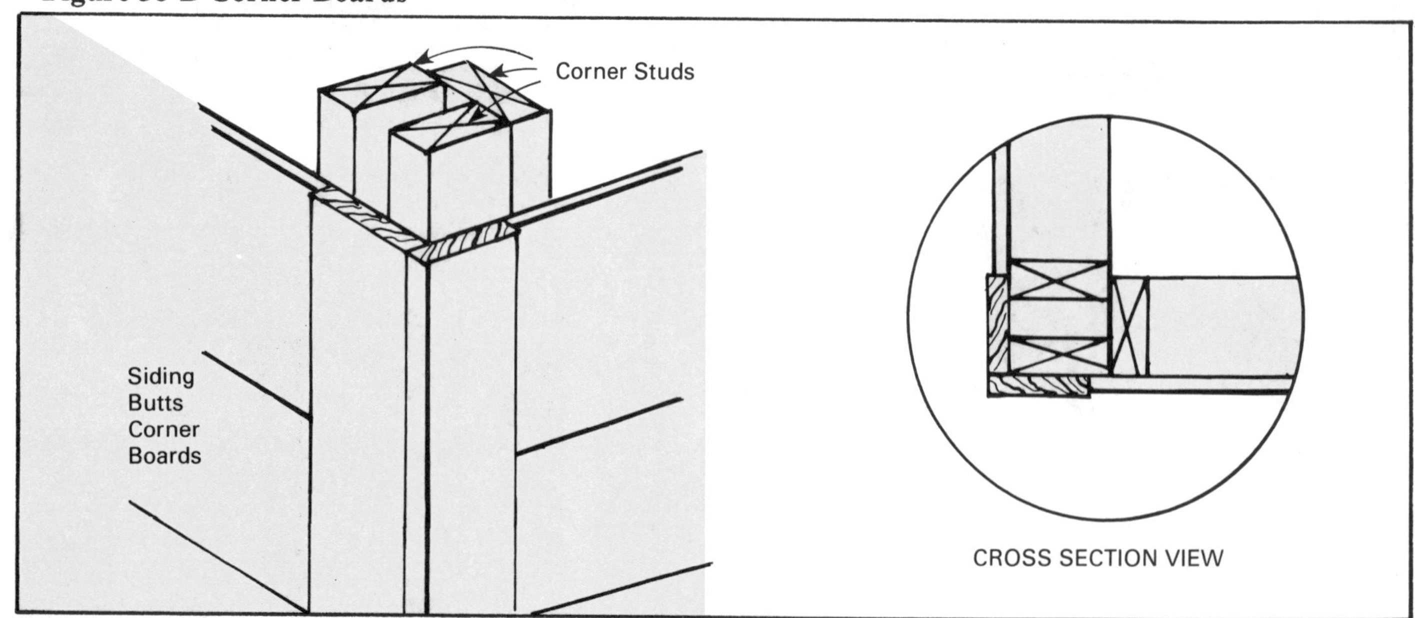

Figure 38-C Inset Corner Boards

Window and Door Details

Study the typical window and door details shown in Figures 39-A through 39-D for examples of door and window framing construction. Because of the great variety in window manufacturing, it is best to study the window manufacturer's installation details before framing and trimming them. Small storage sheds can utilize a built on-site door constructed from plywood and 1by trim (Figure 39-C). Other shed designs with greater traffic should use an exterior prehung door complete with threshold and side and head jambs (Figures 39-A and 39-B).

Figure 39-D illustrates the installation of a metal framed window with nail-on flange. These windows are inexpensive, readily available, and relatively easy to install. Consult the manufacturer's installation instructions for precise step-by-step procedures.

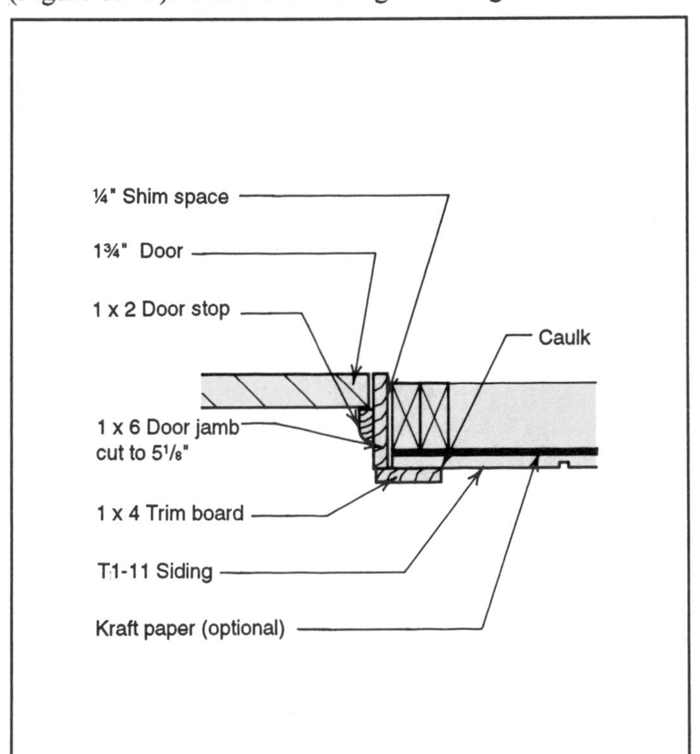

Figure 39-A Service Door Jamb Detail

Figure 39-C Built On-Site Barn Door

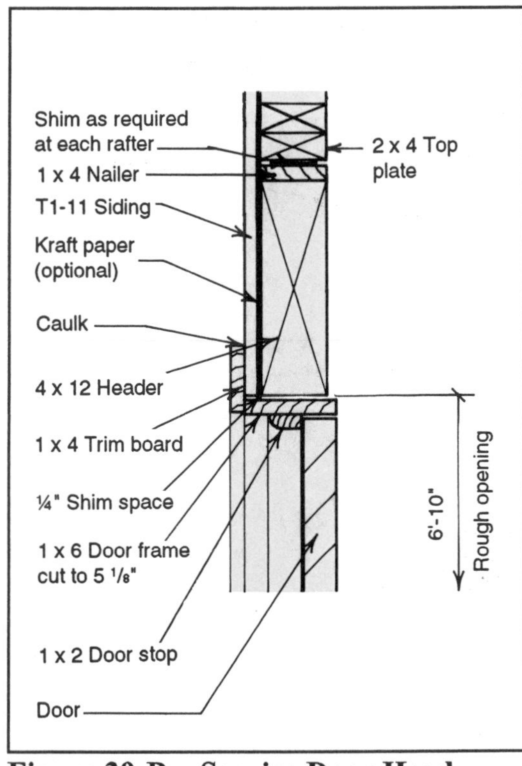

Figure 39-B Service Door Head

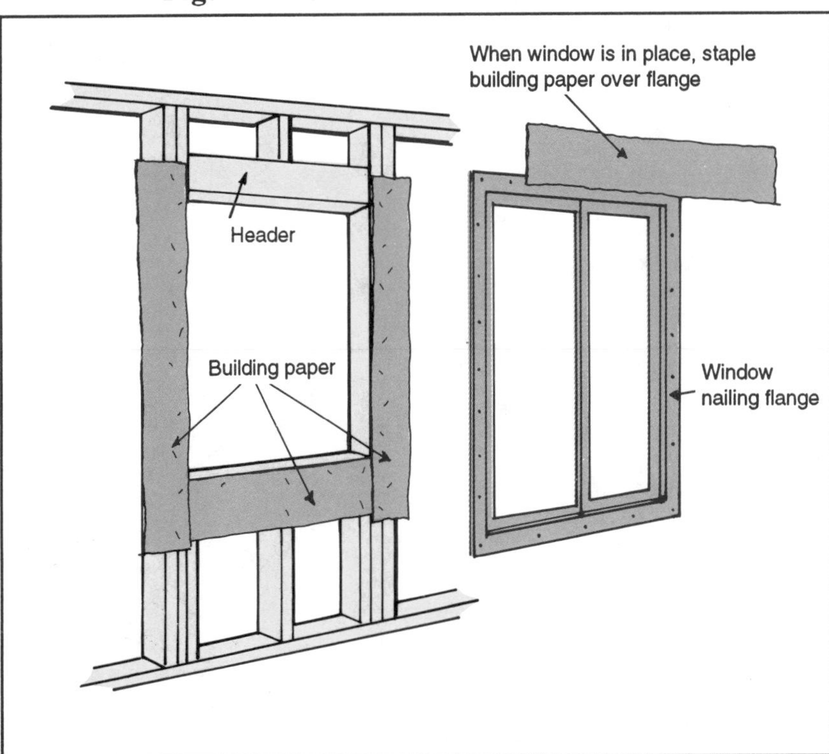

Figure 39-D Metal-Framed Window Installation

Roof Shingles

Once the roof sheathing, cornice trim, and fascia boards are in place, the roof shingles can be applied. See the shingle manufacturer's instructions on the bundle. Shingles chosen to harmonize with or match your home are recommended. Square butt shingles are 36" x 12" in size, have three tabs, and are normally laid with 5" exposed to the weather (Figure 40-A).

Start with 15# asphalt felt paper at the bottom edge of the roof. Lap each course 2". After the roofing felt is on, apply a starter course of shingles (shingles turned upside down), lapping over the eave and rake fascia ½" to provide a drip edge. Use four nails to each shingle and apply a Boston ridge at top which is made by cutting a shingle into thirds (Figure 40-B). Start at one end of the ridge and fasten with two nails to a shingle leaving a 5" exposure. Cut shingles with a utility knife. Metal drip edges are used in some regions.

For a simple-to-install shed roof, use panel roofing (Figure 40-C). Be sure to overhang the eave by at least 2" and install a ridge cap. You can insert one or two translucent fiberglass roof panels between the solid metal roof panels to provide for natural lighting.

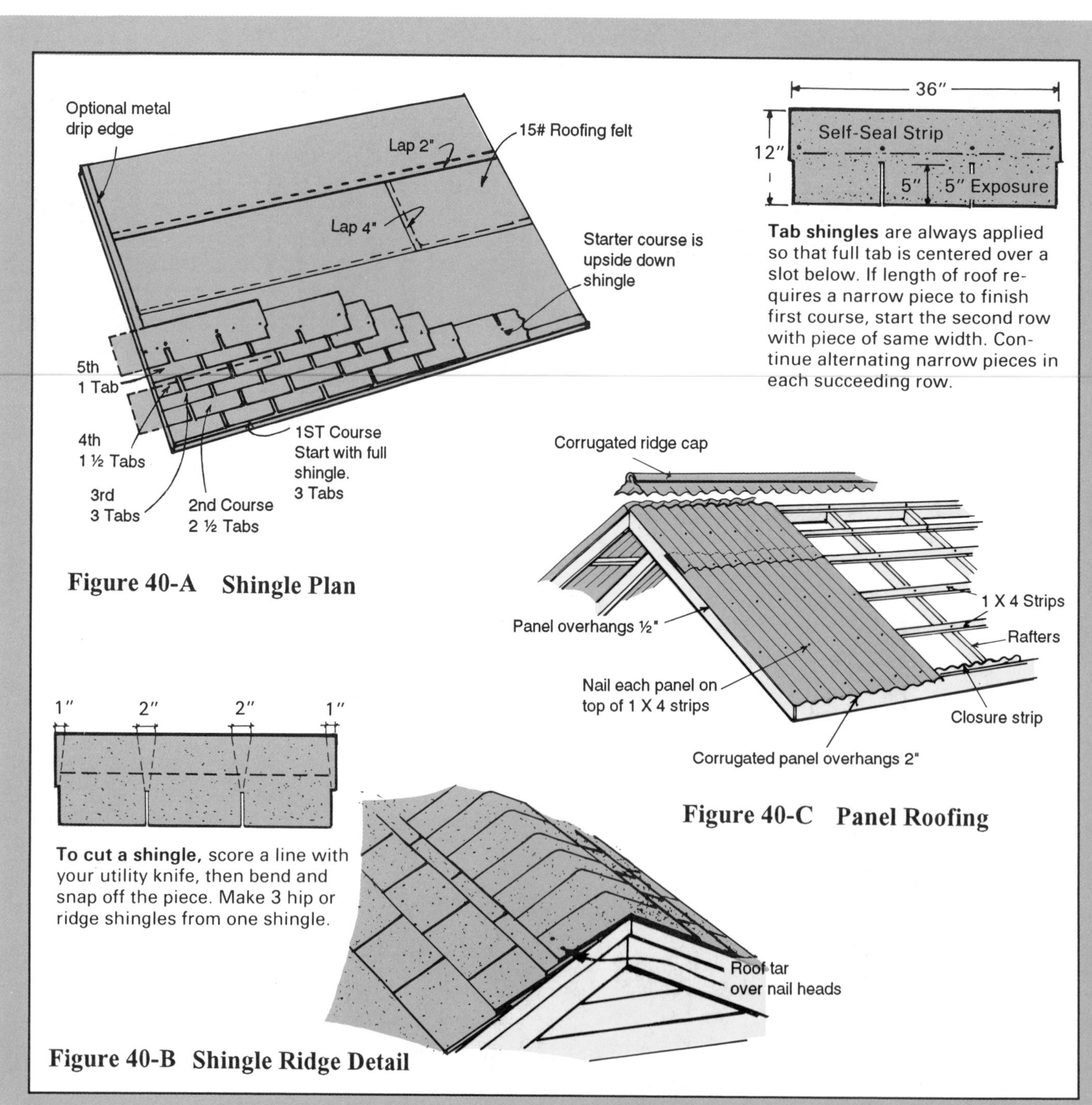

Figure 40-A Shingle Plan

Figure 40-C Panel Roofing

Figure 40-B Shingle Ridge Detail

Installing Electrical Wiring

Depending on how you are going to utilize your shed, you might want to install electrical wiring. Two steps are almost mandatory if you plan to supply your shed with electrical service and want to do the job yourself:

1. First check with your local building department and determine the code standards for your area. They will advise you regarding permit and inspection requirements. They will also advise you whether or not there are any requirements for using a professional electrician during wiring.

2. Consult with your local power company. They will inform you if you need a separate electrical service for your shed. If you plan on running off existing home service, they will tell you if your home service can carry the additional load.

If you are allowed to use a branch circuit from your main panel, install an additional GFCI type circuit breaker in your main circuit box and then use buried cable (Type UF cable for underground burial) to supply your shed. Be certain that you bury the cable in an area that will not be disturbed by digging or other activity. Certain municipalities might not allow buried cable and will require a separate service installation.

You should install a main disconnect box for electrical service inside your shed. Be sure not to exceed the total amperage rating of the box in your branch circuits. Inside the shed you can wire lighting and receptacles using either romex (Type NM cable) or metal sheathed cable (Type BX cable) depending upon your local code requirements. If you are wiring a moist area such as a greenhouse or cabana, use Type NMC cable or Type UM for extra protection against moisture. Also install Ground Fault Circuit Interrupter (GFCI) receptacles in areas with excessive moisture. Consult your local building department for GFCI requirements and regulations.

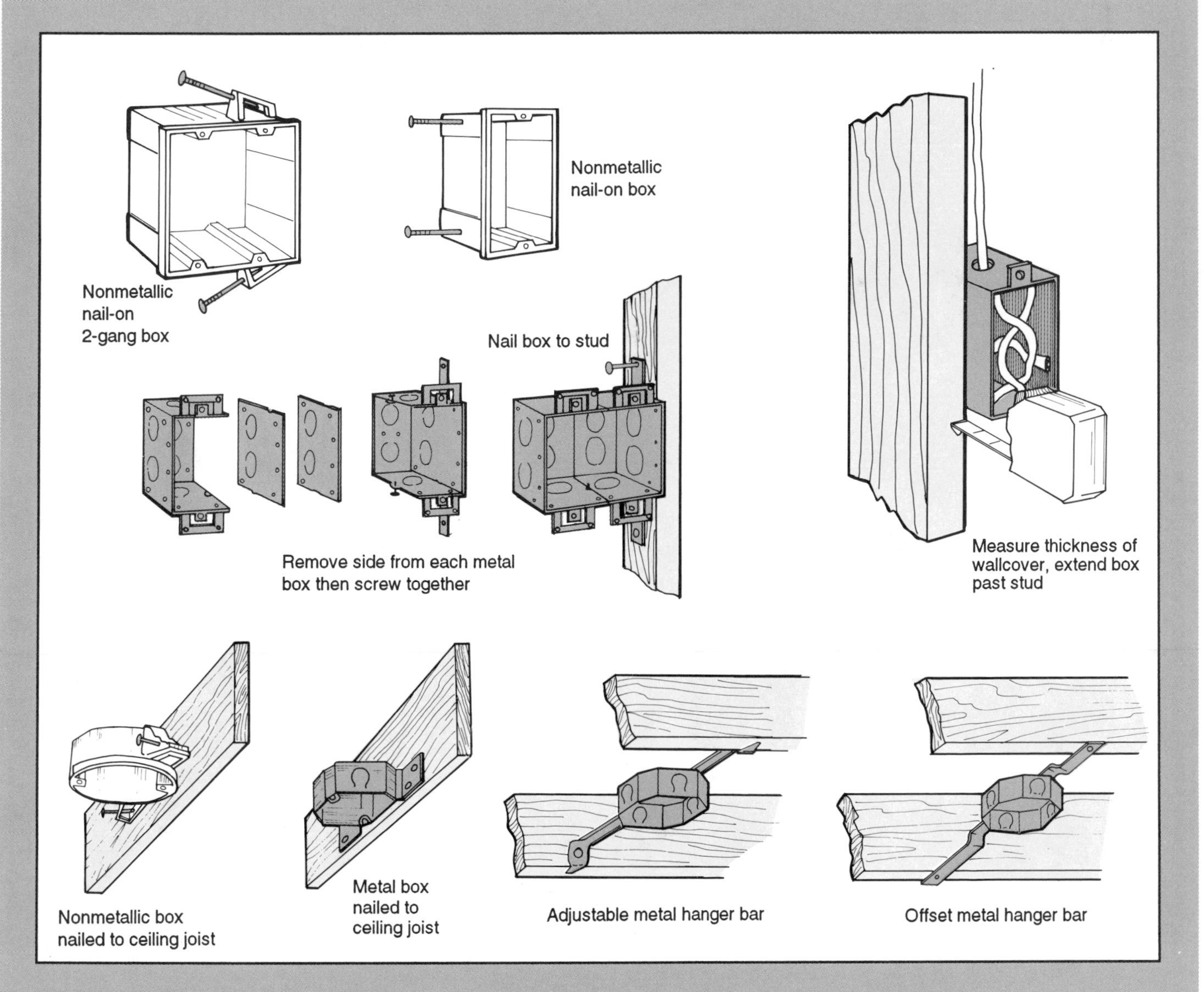

Finishing the Inside of Your Shed

You can either finish the interior of your shed with drywall or leave the wall studs exposed and use blocking to build shelving between the studs. Most shed builders will want to take advantage of the extra storage space afforded by the open wall sections. Use your imagination to create additional storage space by nailing or screwing 1x2 cleats to the studs and then installing extended horizontal shelving over the cleats.

If you elect to install 4' x 8' drywall panels (also known as wallboard) in your shed, study the illustrations below for suggestions on nailing or gluing drywall to wall studs.

A variety of fasteners are available for wallboard. Consult your local home center or building material supplier for suggestions. After you have installed the panels, you can tape and fill the joints with joint compound or simply cover the joints with tape if the final appearance is not a major concern.

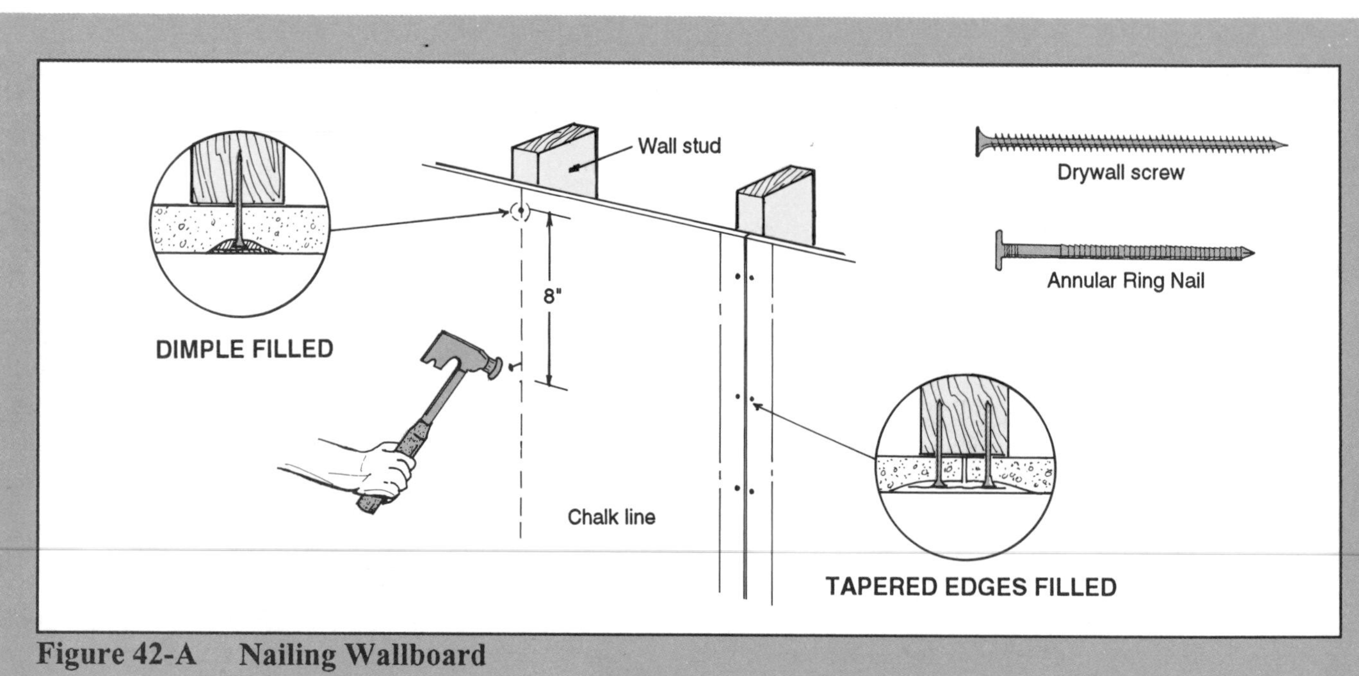

Figure 42-A Nailing Wallboard

Figure 42-B Gluing Wallboard

Adding a Ramp to your Shed

An entry ramp makes life easier for you and your shed. Instead of lugging heavy garden tools such as mowers or snow removal machines up and down from ground level to shed level, use a ramp built from solid 2by material to improve accessibility. If your ramp will be over 3 feet in width, add an additional 2by vertical support to the center of the ramp. Nail the ramp decking to the ramp supports with 12d hot-dipped galvanized nails or use 3" decking screws.

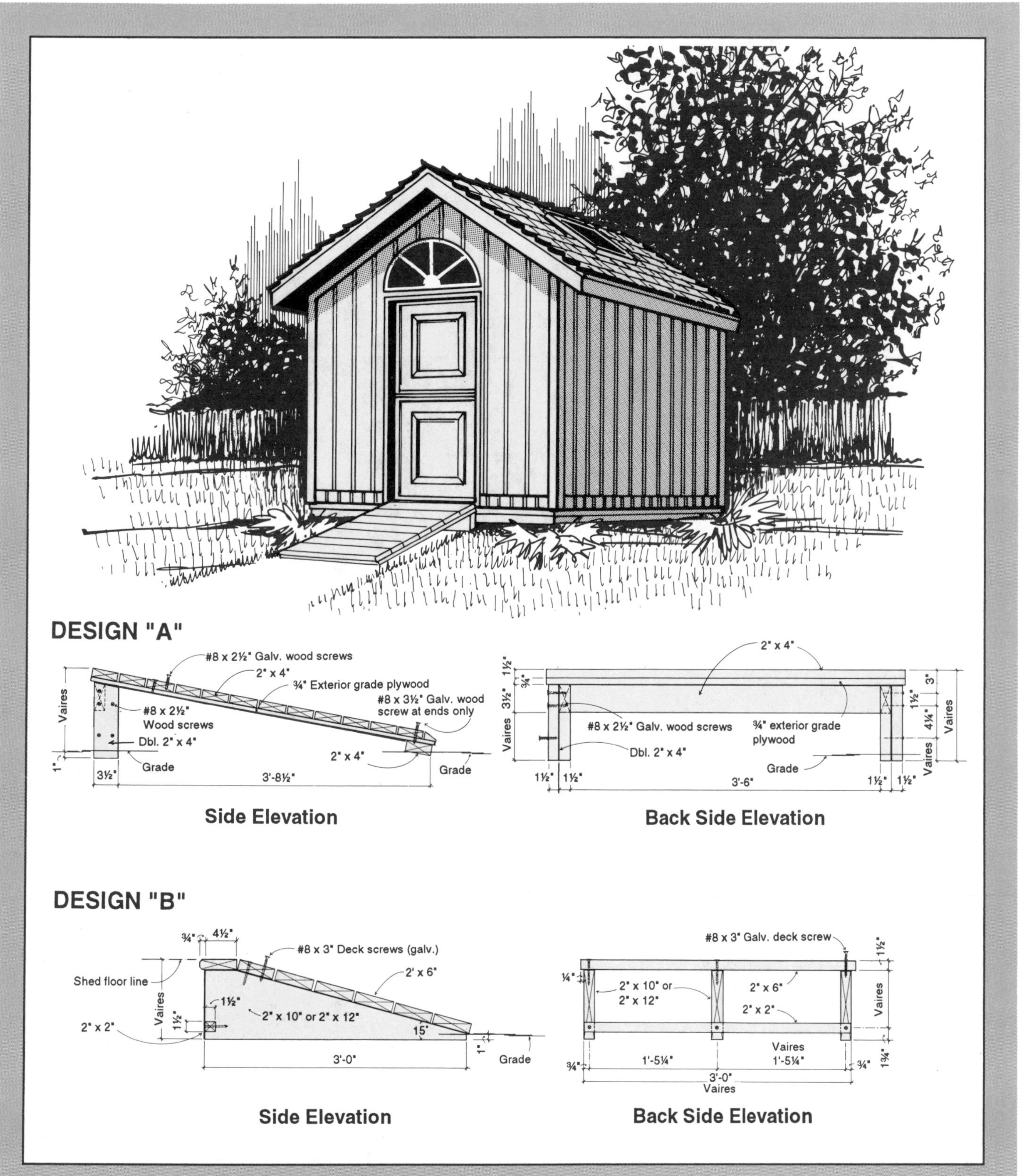

Figure 43-A Ramp Construction Details

Ready to Start Serious Planning?

Now that you have read this book from cover to cover, you're ready to start serious planning. As you can see, there are many details to consider, and they all tie together for successful completion of your shed project.

If the procedures appear at first confusing, reread the information outlined in this book several times before deciding which phases of construction you want to handle yourself and which might require professional assistance.

Because drawing up your own plan from scratch can be time consuming and difficult for the inexperienced builder, you might want to make planning and cost estimating easier by selecting a design from those shown in this book.

If blueprints with lumber lists are not immediately available from your building material dealer, you can order them by using the order form in the back of this book. If after reviewing the blueprints you still have questions, talk them over with your lumber dealer. Most dealers are familiar with construction and will be glad to help you.

The following 17 pages include an assortment of shed plans and shed-related plans. Remember that construction blueprints can be obtained from your dealer or by using the order form on page 64. All blueprint plans include a complete material list, exterior elevations, sections and details, and step-by-step instructions for the successful completion of your shed project.

Example of a Typical Project Plan Sheet

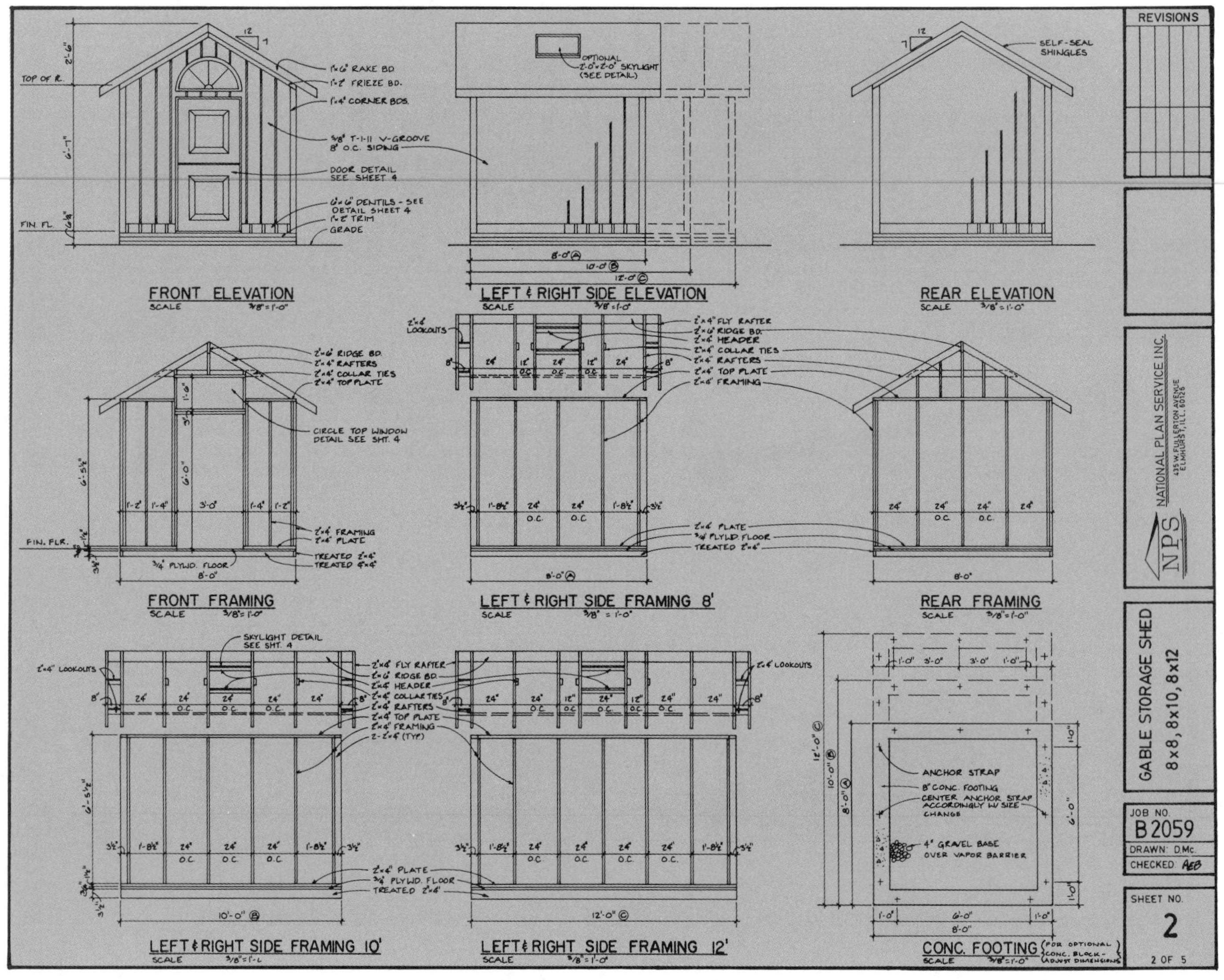

Shed and Other Outdoor Structure Plans

Complete Blueprint Plans are Available for All the Following Plans:

Design

B2001

Little Barn Storage Unit

- Plans detailed for four shed sizes
  7′-3″ wide x 6′ deep
  7′-3″ wide x 8′ deep
  7′-3″ wide x 10′ deep
  7′-3″ wide x 12′ deep
- Height floor to peak 9′-0″
- An attractive addition to your yard
- Storage for dad or playhouse for the kids
- Large, professional easy-to-follow blueprints
- Complete list of materials
- Dimensional drawing of every detail

Design

B2004

Salt Box Storage Shed

- Plans detailed for three shed sizes
  8′ wide x 8′ deep
  12′ wide x 8′ deep
  16′ wide x 8′ deep
- Height floor to peak 8′-2″
- Salt box design
- Wide door opening
- Ideal storage for garden or patio equipment
- Large, professional easy-to-follow blueprints.
- Complete list of materials
- Dimensional drawing of every detail

Design

B2009

Garden Storage Shelter

- Measures 12′ x 10′ x 10′ at peak
- An ideal unit for garden storage
- Also ideal size for camp or retreat shelter
- Made of cedar plywood with battens
- Requires little upkeep
- Large, professional easy-to-follow blueprints.
- Complete list of materials
- Wood cutting diagrams to help you cut cost
- Dimensional drawing of every detail

Design

B2042

Barn Storage Shed with Loft

- Plans detailed for three shed sizes
  12′ wide x 12′ deep
  12′ wide x 16′ deep
  12′ wide x 20′ deep
- Height floor to peak 11′-10″
- Gambrel roof design
- Generous storage space
- Double door for easy access
- Large, professional easy-to-follow blueprints
- Complete list of materials
- Dimensional drawing of every detail

Design

B2054

Barn Storage Shed

- Plans detailed for three shed sizes
  12′ wide x 8′ deep
  12′ wide x 12′ deep
  12′ wide x 16′ deep
- Height floor to peak 9′-4″
- Gambrel roof design
- Generous storage space
- Double door for easy access
- Large, professional easy-to-follow blueprints
- Complete list of materials
- Dimensional drawing of every detail

Design

B2059

Gable Storage Shed

- Plans detailed for three shed sizes
  8′ wide x 8′ deep
  8′ wide x 10′ deep
  8′ wide x 12′ deep
- Height floor to peak 9′-0″
- Gable roof design
- Simple construction
- Circle top window with dutch door
- Large, professional easy-to-follow blueprints.
- Complete list of materials
- Dimensional drawing of every detail

Design

B2061

Contemporary Garden Shed

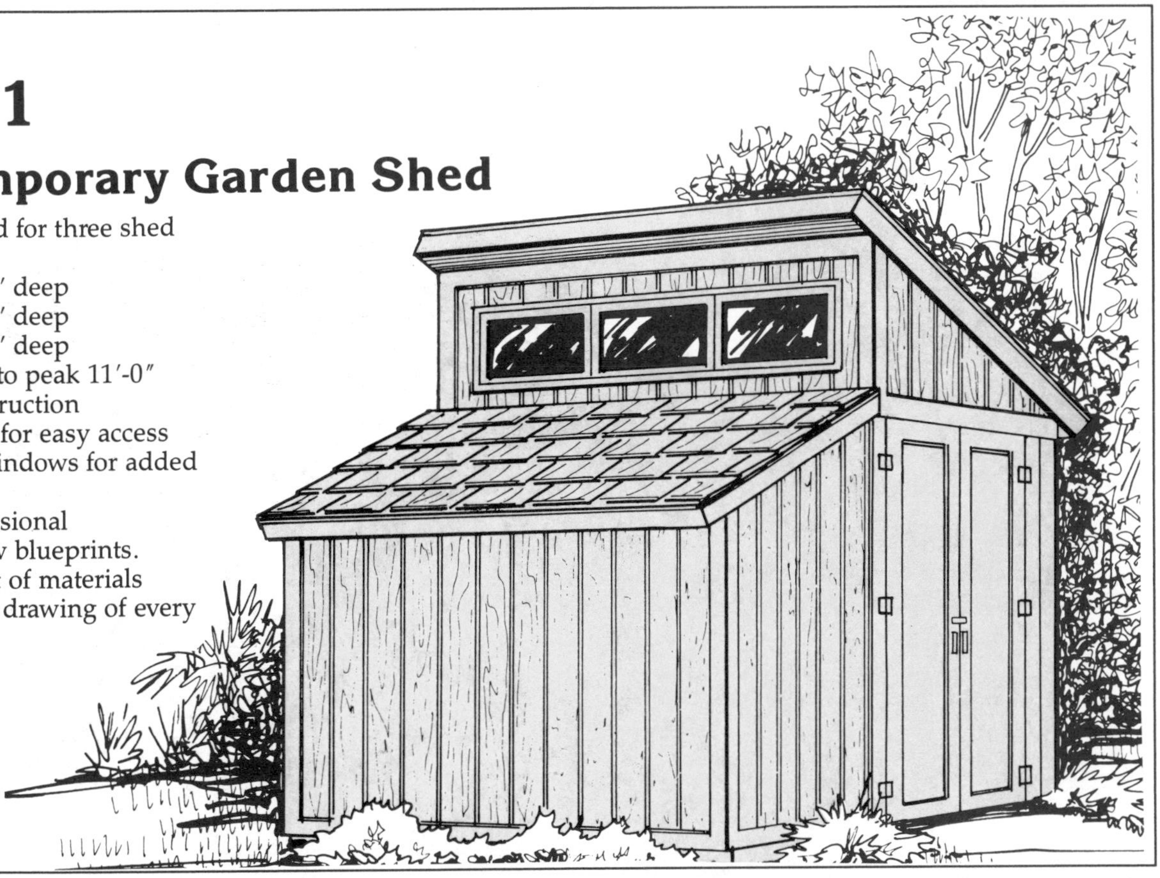

- Plans detailed for three shed sizes
  10′ wide x 10′ deep
  12′ wide x 10′ deep
  14′ wide x 10′ deep
- Height floor to peak 11′-0″
- Simple construction
- Double door for easy access
- Clerestory windows for added light
- Large, professional easy-to-follow blueprints.
- Complete list of materials
- Dimensional drawing of every detail

Design

X6028

Convenience Shed

- Size 16'-0" x 12'-0" x 12'-4" high
- Boxed bay area ideal for potting plants.
- 80 Sq. Ft. of bonus storage in attic.
- Large, professional easy-to-follow blueprints.
- List of materials.
- Dimensional drawings and details.

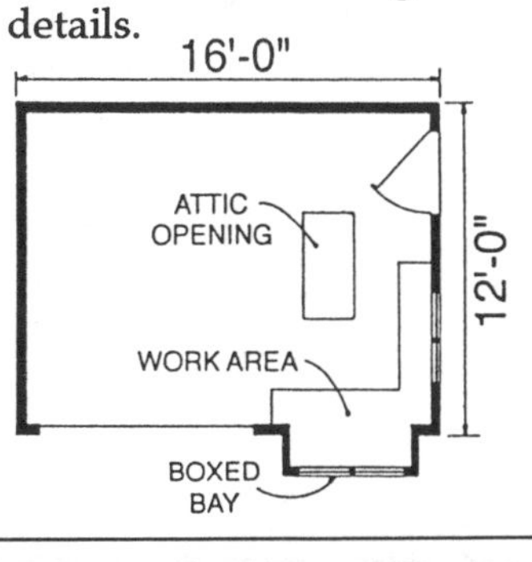

16'-0"
ATTIC OPENING
WORK AREA
BOXED BAY
12'-0"

Design

B2064

Log / Storage Shed

- Peak to grade height 10′-0″
- Storage Area 7′-6″ x 6′-0″
- Log storage area 2′-6″ x 6′-0″
- Overall Dimension 10′ x 6′
- Adds value and beauty to your home.
- Unique, attractive design.
- Can be built with standard lumber.
- Large, professional easy-to-follow blueprints.
- Complete list of materials
- Dimensional drawing of every detail

UCANDO Patterns

U00800

8′ Wide Budget Barn

- Floor Size 88-5/16″ Wide x 92″ Long
- Door Size 42-7/8″ Wide x 6′ High
- Building Height 8′ High
- Detailed material list
- Easy to read instruction sheet
- Sturdy reusable templates
- Cutting layout sheet

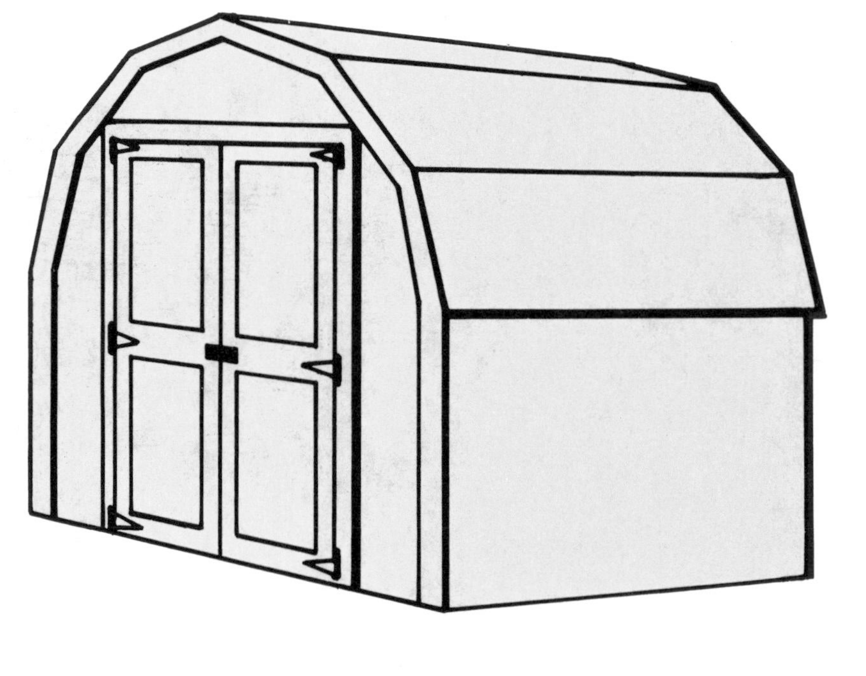

UCANDO Patterns

U00810

10′ Wide Barn

- Floor Size 10′ Wide x 116″ Deep
- Door Size 8′ Wide x 6′ High
- Building Height 8′ High
- Detailed material list
- Easy to read instruction sheet
- Sturdy reusable templates
- Cutting layout sheet

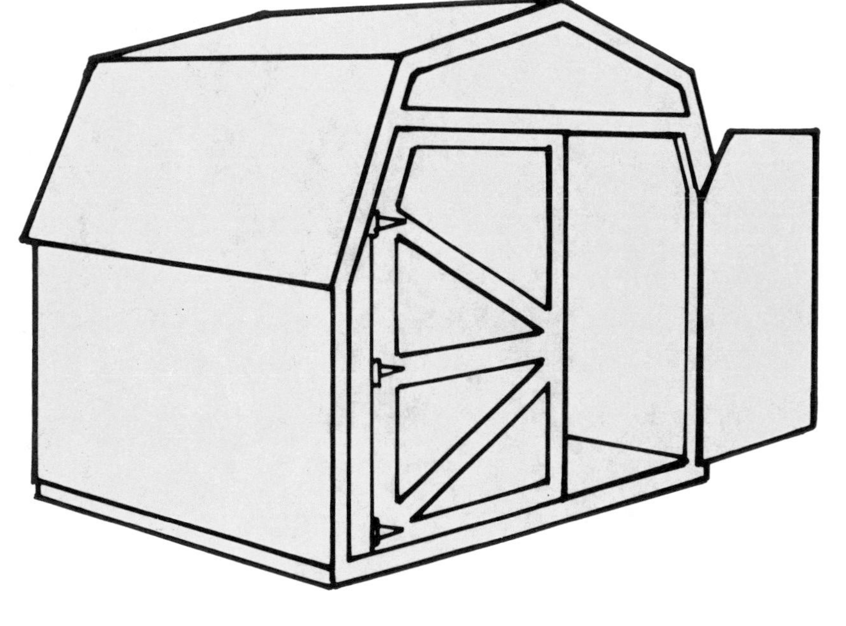

UCANDO Patterns

U00812

12′ Wide Barn

- Floor Size 12′ Wide x 11′-6″ deep
- Door Size 8′ Wide x 6′ High
- Building Height 8′ High
- Detailed material list
- Easy to read instruction sheet
- Sturdy reusable templates
- Cutting layout sheet

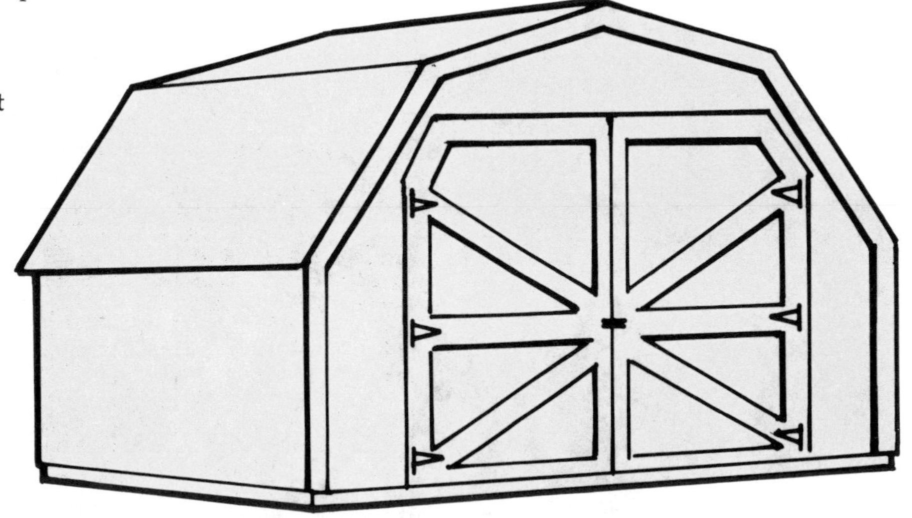

Design

B2022

Storage Shed Playhouse

- Size: 8′-0″ x 12′-0″
- Quaint chalet design
- Ideal playhouse in summer
- Storage shed in the off season
- Large, professional easy-to-follow blueprints.
- Complete list of materials
- Dimensional drawing of every detail

Design

B2044

Storage Shed with Playhouse

- Size: 12′-0″ x 14′-8″ x 14′-2″ high
- A storage shed for dad . . . and a playhouse for the kids . . . above.
- Separate entrance for storage and playhouse . . . kids climb the ladder to playhouse entrance on upper level.
- Simple construction.
- Large, professional easy-to-follow blueprints
- Complete list of materials
- Dimensional drawing of every detail

Design

B2071

Children's Playhouse

- Size 6′-0″ x 6′-0″ x 7′-2″ high
- Give the kids a place of their own
- Victorian Style Playhouse
- Simple construction. . . fun to do!
- Large, professional easy-to-follow blueprints.
- Complete list of materials
- Dimensional drawing of every detail

UCANDO Patterns

U00320

Playhouse

- 6′ x 6′ Playhouse
- Floor Size 6′ Wide x 6′ Deep
- Door size 24″ Wide x 45-1/2″ High
- Building Height 62-1/2″ High
- From this one template you can trace all the parts to make your playhouse
- Detailed material list
- Easy to read instruction sheet
- Sturdy reusable templates
- Cutting layout sheet

Design

B2031

Greenhouse-Storage

- Large size 12′ x 8′ x 8′
- Store lawn and garden tools right at hand
- An attractive addition to your yard
- Large, professional easy-to-follow blueprints.
- Complete list of materials

Design

B2033

Greenhouse Storage Shed

- Size: 10 ft. wide x 8 ft. deep x 8 ft. high
- Plastic side panels allow for use as a greenhouse
- Attractive double duty storage shed
- Large, professional easy-to-follow blueprints
- Complete list of materials
- Dimensional drawing of every detail

Design

B2083

Greenhouse

- Size 10'-0" x 12'-0" x 10'-0" high
- An attractive addition to your yard.
- Large, professional easy-to-follow blueprints.
- Complete list of materials.
- Dimensional drawing of every detail.
- Rafter cutting template.

UCANDO Patterns

U00150

8' Greenhouse

- Size 8'-0" x 7'-6" x 8'-0" high
- Detailed material list
- Easy to read instruction sheet
- Sturdy reusable templates
- Cutting layout sheet

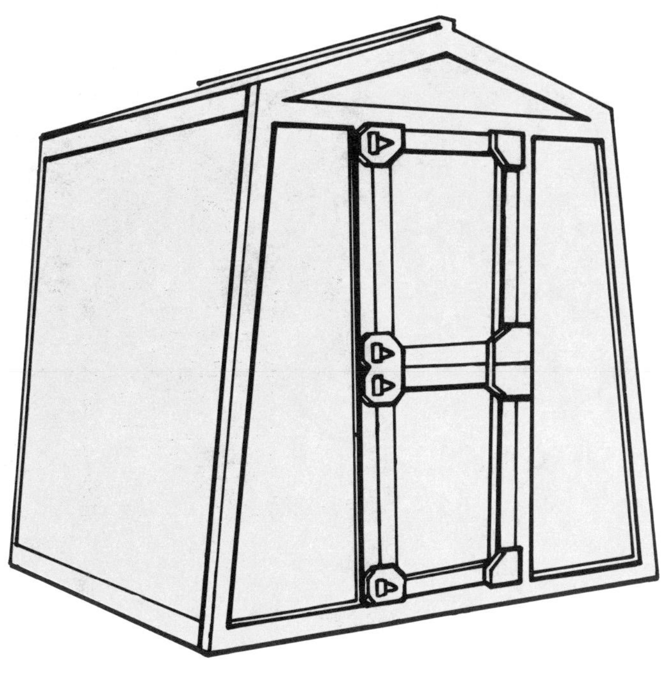

Design

B2023

Yard or Pool Side Storage and Cabana

- Size: 16′-0″ x 8′-0″
- Unique mansard roof design
- Convenient dressing room
- Storage for poolside furniture & equipt.
- Large, professional easy-to-follow blueprints.
- Complete list of materials
- Dimensional drawing of every detail

Design

B2080

Deluxe Cabana

- Size 11'-0" x 13'-6"
- Unique roof design.
- Convenient dressing room and servicing area.
- Storage for poolside furniture & equiptment
- Large, professional easy-to-follow blueprints.
- Complete list of materials.
- Dimensional drawing of every detail.
- Rafter cutting template.

Design
B2066
Patio Cover

- Designed for two sizes: 12'wide x 12'deep or 16'wide x 12'deep
- Designed to cover an existing deck or patio, or may be used as a pavilion
- Unique design
- Free standing structure
- Can be built with standard lumber
- Simple construction
- Plan detailed with an alternate bench design
- Large, professional easy-to-follow blueprints
- Complete list of materials
- Dimensional drawing of every detail

Design
B2068
Easy Patio Cover

- Size 16'wide x 12'deep
- Unique attractive patio cover features a sun screen covering
- Add value and beauty to your home
- Simple construction
- Large, professional easy-to-follow blueprints
- Complete list of materials
- Dimensional drawing of every detail

Design

B2072

Garden Entryway

- Size 8′-0″ x 8′-0″
- Peak to grade height 10′-10$^{1}/_{4}$″
- Simple construction
- Unique, attractive design that will complement either your garden or home.
- Large, professional easy-to-follow blueprints.
- List of materials.
- Dimensional drawings and details.

Design

B2074

6-Sided Gazebo

- Size: 9′-2″ x 8′-0″
- Unique, attractive design that will complement either your garden or home.
- Add value and beauty to your home
- Simple construction
- Large, professional easy-to-follow blueprints.
- List of materials.
- Dimensional drawings and details.

Design

X6027

Octo-Gazebo

- Size 12'-0" x 12'-0" x 17'-0" high
- Build yourself a summer place out of the sun.
- Large, professional easy-to-follow blueprints.
- List of materials.
- Dimensional drawings and details.

Design

X6016

Pole Building Open Shed

- Size 13'-0" x 36'-0" - 8' or 10' front
- The building can be lengthened by adding as many 12' bays as required.
- Expandable
- Simple Construction
- Large, professional easy-to-follow blueprints.
- List of materials.
- Dimensional drawings and details.

UCANDO® PROJECT PLANS

All plans are easy-to-follow and fully detailed. A complete list of material included.

B2056 13'x13'x10' high
Wooden Swings

B2041 8' x 8'
Jungle Gym

B2072 8' x 8'
Garden Entryway

B2067 Canopy 12'-0" x 5'-0" x 7'6" Bench 6'-0" Long
Garden Swing

B2061 10' x 10' 12' x 10' 14' x 10'
Contemporary Garden Shed

B2064 10' x 6'
Log Storage Shed

B2071 6'-0" x 6'-0" x 7'2"
Children's Playhouse

B2025
Two Doghouses

B2042 12' x 12' x 11'10" 12' x 16' x 11'10" 12' x 20' x 11'10"
Storage Shed

B2004 8' x 8' x 8'2" 12' x 8' x 8'2" 16' x 8' x 8'2"
Storage Barn

B2059 8' x 8' 8' x 10' 8' x 12'
Gable Storage Shed

B2054 12' x 8' x 9'4" 12' x 12' x 9'4" 12' x 16' x 9'4"
Storage Shed

A100—PROJECT PLANS—contains more than 155 do-it-yourself projects you can build—includes garages, gazebos, decks, storage sheds, pole buildings, horse barns, furniture and children's projects.

BLUEPRINT ORDER FORM

- When you're ready to order construction blueprints we recommend that you order them from the dealer who provided this book.
- Your dealer can give you valuable and cost-saving information about local building code requirements and the availability of local contractors and financing should you so require.
- Take advantage of your dealer's knowledge and experience!

BLUEPRINT ORDER FORM

NATIONAL PLAN SERVICE
DEPT. A210
435 WEST FULLERTON AVENUE
ELMHURST, ILLINOIS 60126-1498
PHONE TOLL FREE 1-800-533-4350 IN ILLINOIS 1-708-833-0640 FAX ORDER 1-800-344-4293

NPS

ALL PRICES SUBJECT TO CHANGE WITHOUT NOTICE NOT RETURNABLE

PLEASE RUSH ME THE ITEMS CHECKED BELOW

☐ **A100** Project Plan Book **$4.95**

Item	Price	Item	Price	Item	Price	Item	Price
☐ **B2001** Little Barn Storage Unit	**$5.95**	☐ **B2042** Barn Storage Shed	**$5.95**	☐ **B2068** Easy Patio Cover	**$5.95**	☐ **X6027** Octo-Gazebo	**$12.95**
☐ **B2004** Salt Box Storage Shed	**$5.95**	☐ **B2044** Storage Shed / Playhouse	**$5.95**	☐ **B2071** Children's Playhouse	**$5.95**	☐ **X6028** Convenience Shed	**$12.95**
☐ **B2009** Garden Storage Shelter	**$5.95**	☐ **B2054** Barn Storage Shed	**$5.95**	☐ **B2072** Garden Entryway	**$5.95**	☐ **U00150** Greenhouse	**$14.95**
☐ **B2022** Storage Shed Playhouse	**$5.95**	☐ **B2059** Gable Storage Shed	**$5.95**	☐ **B2074** 6 Sided Gazebo	**$5.95**	☐ **U00320** Playhouse	**$6.95**
☐ **B2023** Yard/Pool Storage & Cabana	**$5.95**	☐ **B2061** Contemporary Storage Shed	**$5.95**	☐ **B2080** Deluxe Cabana	**$5.95**	☐ **U00800** 8' Wide Budget Barn	**$10.95**
☐ **B2031** Greenhouse-Storage	**$5.95**	☐ **B2064** Log / Storage Shed	**$5.95**	☐ **B2083** Greenhouse	**$5.95**	☐ **U00810** 10' Wide Barn	**$14.95**
☐ **B2033** Greenhouse-Storage Shed	**$5.95**	☐ **B2066** Patio Covers	**$5.95**	☐ **X6016** Open Utility Shed	**$12.95**	☐ **U00812** 12' Wide Barn	**$14.95**

☐ Payment is enclosed (check or money order)
☐ Please charge to my credit card below

SALES TAX Illinois Residents please add 7% sales tax.
AL,CA,MD,OH,TN,and PA Please add appropriate sales tax.

TOTAL ...... $______
TAX (see tax note) ...... $______
Shipping and Handling charges ...... $ **2.00**
TOTAL ORDER ...... $______

USE CREDIT CARDS ONLY FOR $10.00 OR MORE - U.S. ONLY

MasterCard ☐ If you wish to use your charge card, check box at left and fill out boxes below.
VISA ☐ Expiration Date Month/Year______

Credit Card No.______

Name ______
Address ______
City ______ State____ Zip____
Phone ( )______

BLUEPRINT ORDER FORM

NATIONAL PLAN SERVICE
DEPT. A210
435 WEST FULLERTON AVENUE
ELMHURST, ILLINOIS 60126-1498
PHONE TOLL FREE 1-800-533-4350 IN ILLINOIS 1-708-833-0640 FAX ORDER 1-800-344-4293

NPS

ALL PRICES SUBJECT TO CHANGE WITHOUT NOTICE NOT RETURNABLE

PLEASE RUSH ME THE ITEMS CHECKED BELOW

☐ **A100** Project Plan Book **$4.95**

Item	Price	Item	Price	Item	Price	Item	Price
☐ **B2001** Little Barn Storage Unit	**$5.95**	☐ **B2042** Barn Storage Shed	**$5.95**	☐ **B2068** Easy Patio Cover	**$5.95**	☐ **X6027** Octo-Gazebo	**$12.95**
☐ **B2004** Salt Box Storage Shed	**$5.95**	☐ **B2044** Storage Shed / Playhouse	**$5.95**	☐ **B2071** Children's Playhouse	**$5.95**	☐ **X6028** Convenience Shed	**$12.95**
☐ **B2009** Garden Storage Shelter	**$5.95**	☐ **B2054** Barn Storage Shed	**$5.95**	☐ **B2072** Garden Entryway	**$5.95**	☐ **U00150** Greenhouse	**$14.95**
☐ **B2022** Storage Shed Playhouse	**$5.95**	☐ **B2059** Gable Storage Shed	**$5.95**	☐ **B2074** 6 Sided Gazebo	**$5.95**	☐ **U00320** Playhouse	**$6.95**
☐ **B2023** Yard/Pool Storage & Cabana	**$5.95**	☐ **B2061** Contemporary Storage Shed	**$5.95**	☐ **B2080** Deluxe Cabana	**$5.95**	☐ **U00800** 8' Wide Budget Barn	**$10.95**
☐ **B2031** Greenhouse-Storage	**$5.95**	☐ **B2064** Log / Storage Shed	**$5.95**	☐ **B2083** Greenhouse	**$5.95**	☐ **U00810** 10' Wide Barn	**$14.95**
☐ **B2033** Greenhouse-Storage Shed	**$5.95**	☐ **B2066** Patio Covers	**$5.95**	☐ **X6016** Open Utility Shed	**$12.95**	☐ **U00812** 12' Wide Barn	**$14.95**

☐ Payment is enclosed (check or money order)
☐ Please charge to my credit card below

SALES TAX Illinois Residents please add 7% sales tax.
AL,CA,MD,OH,TN,and PA Please add appropriate sales tax.

TOTAL ...... $______
TAX (see tax note) ...... $______
Shipping and Handling charges ...... $ **2.00**
TOTAL ORDER ...... $______

USE CREDIT CARDS ONLY FOR $10.00 OR MORE - U.S. ONLY

MasterCard ☐ If you wish to use your charge card, check box at left and fill out boxes below.
VISA ☐ Expiration Date Month/Year______

Credit Card No.______

Name ______
Address ______
City ______ State____ Zip____
Phone ( )______

YOU MAY PHOTOCOPY THIS ORDER FORM